ANTI-SEMITISM
IN THE UNITED STATES

ANTI-SEMITISM IN THE UNITED STATES

A Study of Prejudice in the 1980s

Gregory Martire and Ruth Clark

PRAEGER

PRAEGER SPECIAL STUDIES • PRAEGER SCIENTIFIC

Library of Congress Cataloging in Publication Data

Martire, Gregory.
  Anti-Semitism in the United States.

  Bibliography: p.
  Includes index.
  1. Antisemitism—United States.   2. United States—
Ethnic relations.   I. Clark, Ruth (Ruth V.)   II. Title.
DS146.U6M325   1982   305.8′924′073   82-13264
ISBN 0-03-061907-6

305.8
M386a

Published in 1982 by Praeger Publishers
CBS Educational and Professional Publishing
a Division of CBS Inc.
521 Fifth Avenue, New York, New York 10175, U.S.A.

© 1982 by Praeger Publishers

83-3985   23456789   052   987654321

Printed in the United States of America

PREFACE

When one studies the extent of anti-Semitism, or for that matter the contributions that Jews have made to American culture, it is sometimes easy to lose sight of the fact that Jews represent less than 3 percent of the total population of the United States. Despite the abhorrence one might feel toward any form of prejudice, the size of the U.S. Jewish community raises the question, why pay special attention to this particular type of prejudice?

The special concern stems from at least two sources. First, the lengthy history of anti-Semitism, and particularly the experience of the Holocaust, makes anti-Semitic prejudice more of a focus of moral outrage than other types of prejudice. Second, and perhaps equally important, is the fact that, to paraphrase Dostoevsky, a civilization can be judged by its treatment of Jews and other minorities. Long before America was even discovered, a nation's treatment of Jews provided an indication of its tolerance of minorities. The study of anti-Semitism must be understood then, not simply as the study of attitudes toward one small minority group but rather as the study of the character of the culture itself.

The current study attempts to shed light on the level of tolerance in the United States in the 1980s by addressing five basic questions: What has happened to stereotypes of American Jews in recent years? Has the nature of anti-Semitism changed? Does the apparent increase in anti-Semitic incidents in recent years reflect a genuine increase in anti-Semitism? Has the increased acceptance of diverse views and values that characterized the United States in the 1960s and 1970s resulted in increased acceptance of Jews? Is the United States more or less tolerant than it was in the early 1960s?

ACKNOWLEDGMENTS

The study reported in this volume was the result of the collaborative efforts of many individuals. First, we owe a debt to the American Jewish Committee both for its sponsorship and for the ideas and assistance provided by Bertram Gold, executive vice president, Milton Himmelfarb, director of information and research services, and Geraldine Rosenfield, researcher.

The study was conducted by Yankelovich, Skelly and White, Inc., and many staff members played critical roles, including Walter Davis, who had responsibility for the computer analysis, Bob Stahlheber, who directed the fieldwork, and Jeff O'Donnell, who designed the sample. In addition, the authors received many helpful comments and suggestions from Kevin Clancy, John Doble, Brian Jones, Mary Martire, Sara Seims, Linda Simons, and Gordon Wyner. Maria Vitucci, who typed the manuscript, performed in her usual able fashion, particularly considering the illegible drafts and revisions with which she worked.

The data utilized for the 1964 baseline in this publication were made available by the Inter-University Consortium for Political and Social Research. The data were originally collected by Gertrude Selznick and Stephen Steinberg.

The responsibility for the analysis and interpretations presented here rests solely with the authors.

CONTENTS

LIST OF TABLES

LIST OF FIGURES

ANTI-SEMITISM
IN THE UNITED STATES

1

INTRODUCTION

On October 4, 1980, a terrorist bomb exploded in front of a Reform temple on the rue Corpernic in Paris, killing four people and injuring an additional twelve. That event and the wave of anti-Semitic incidents that followed in the United States and in many other parts of the world led many observers to question whether anti-Semitism was again on the rise. Indeed, several days after the incident, France's President Giscard D'Estaing wondered aloud on French television whether "anti-Semitism is being reborn in France."[1]

During the same time, the Anti-Defamation League of B'nai B'rith recorded an alarming increase in the number of anti-Semitic incidents in the United States. While reports of the number of such incidents are subject to a variety of interpretations,[2] they nevertheless do raise the question, Is anti-Semitism on the rise after several decades of apparent dormancy?

This concern about the possibility of rising levels of anti-Semitism is not without some historical foundation. Indeed, many of the factors associated with the growth of European anti-Semitism in the 1920s and 1930s have reemerged: economic turmoil, the worst inflation in a generation, a growing militarism, an increase in political conservatism, and widespread concern about the nation's position in the world. In addition, the last decade has seen an increase in the visibility and the political power of religious fundamentalists in the United States and other parts of the world.

While Jews have served as scapegoats for economic, political, and religious turmoil throughout history, the present epoch brings one new dimension to this age-old problem, the State of Israel. The Middle East is now central to many international economic and political problems. Consequently, the potential always exists for real or imagined conflicts between the interests of the Israelis and those of the United States and other Western nations.

While there are many worrisome signs, there are also solid reasons to believe that anti-Semitism may be on the wane in the United States. Perhaps most important are the indications that the 1960s and 1970s were a time of increased acceptance of social pluralism in the United States. In his recent book, *New Rules*, Daniel Yankelovich describes this increasing social pluralism.

> Over the past several decades, the rules of social behavior have expanded moving us from a society with relatively homogeneous definitions of family, sex roles and working life toward an explosive pluralism on these and other fronts.
>
> Virtually all the recent normative changes in America have moved toward greater tolerance, openness, choice and a wider range of acceptable behavior.[3]

Extrapolating from Yankelovich, one might argue that the growing social pluralism that he describes could be expected to produce an increased tolerance of different outlooks and ways of life and may have reduced the level of intolerance toward Jews and other minority group members. To put the matter more simply: should we not expect to find a lessening of prejudice against Jews and other minorities in a culture that has learned to be increasingly tolerant of other groups of people with different values, life-styles, and backgrounds.[4] This is a theme we shall return to in Chapter 6.

In addition to this growing social pluralism, there are indications that actual discrimination against Jews has declined significantly over the years. One of the most visible indications of change has been the decline in discrimination against Jews in universities and social clubs.

Earlier in this century, Harvard University, that bastion of liberal enlightenment, formally considered the proposal of its president, Lawrence Lowell, to restrict the number of Jews admitted to Harvard College. Ultimately, such a policy was not formally adopted, though restriction of the number of Jews admitted was carried out through informal mechanisms. Such a policy, whether formally or informally established, would be unthinkable today.

More recently, as late as the early 1960s, in his book, *The Protestant Establishment*, E. Digby Baltzell discusses the then not uncommon practice of restricting Jewish membership in country clubs.[5] While clubs that restrict Jews are not unheard of today, they are nevertheless significantly less common. Indeed, as Chapter 11 indicates, only 5 percent of non-Jews and 14 percent of Jews have, in the last year or two, come across clubs or organizations that restrict Jews. While trend data on the subject are not available, it is safe to say that current levels of social club restriction represent a sharp departure from the past in the direction of lower levels of discrimination.

THE PURPOSE OF THE STUDY

The present study was conducted with two overall objectives in mind: first, to provide the first comprehensive trend study of anti-Semitism in the United States,[6] and second, to examine the factors that are associated with American anti-Semitism in the 1980s.

The baseline for the current study is a national survey conducted in 1964 by Gertrude Selznick and Steven Steinberg and published in 1969 as *The Tenacity of Prejudice.*[7] This was part of the five-year study of anti-Semitism sponsored by the Anti-Defamation League of B'nai B'rith and conducted at the University of California at Berkeley. The study was selected because it represents the first comprehensive national survey of anti-Semitism.[8] In addition, the survey findings that bear on attitudes toward Israel made use of a 1977 study conducted for the American Jewish Committee by Yankelovich, Skelly and White, Inc.

THE MAJOR THEMES OF THE STUDY

There are many ways to tell a story. Some prefer to keep their audience in the dark until just before the final curtain; others, such as ourselves, prefer to let the audience know where we are going at the outset so that they can be the judge of the interpretations and conclusions. The major themes of the study that follow provide a summary of the survey results.

While they are a minority, individuals holding anti-Semitic beliefs clearly represent a significant social problem in the United

States. This is supported by the fact that three or more out of ten non-Jews believe that: "Jews stick together too much"; "Jews always like to be at the head of things"; "Jewish employers go out of their way to hire other Jews"; "Jews have too much power in the business world"; "Jews are stubborn and resist change"; and "Jews are more loyal to Israel than to America." The current analysis indicates that one in four (23 percent) non-Jews can be characterized as prejudiced; while just under one out of two (45 percent) are unprejudiced; the remainder (32 percent) are neutral—neither strongly prejudiced nor unprejudiced.[9]

Anti-Semitic incidents are a widespread problem. In 1981 the Anti-Defamation League of B'nai B'rith (ADL) recorded reports of 974 episodes of anti-Semitic vandalism in 31 states and the District of Columbia compared to 377 incidents in 28 states and the District of Columbia in 1980.

While the current survey does not include trend measurements in either awareness of incidents or victimization, it does suggest that such incidents may be much more widespread than the ADL reports would indicate. Indeed, four out of ten non-Jews and the vast majority (79 percent) of Jews say they have been exposed to anti-Semitic incidents in the last year or two where they live or work.

While anti-Semitic beliefs continue to represent a serious social problem, there has been a decline in the prevalence of many traditional anti-Semitic beliefs since 1964. This decline has been more pronounced when it comes to traditional negative stereotypes about Jewish character. For example, since 1964, there has been a decline in the proportion of non-Jews who feel that Jews: have a lot of irritating faults (48 percent in 1964, down to 29 percent in 1981); are more willing to use shady business practices (48 percent in 1964, down to 33 percent in 1981); are shrewd and tricky in business (40 percent in 1964, down to 27 percent in 1981); and are not as honest as other businessmen (34 percent in 1964, down to 22 percent in 1981). (These figures were repercentaged without those who said, "Not sure." See Table 3.1 for percentages based on total sample.)

While the focus of much research about attitudes toward Jews has been on negative images, it is clear that positive images of Jews are more pervasive. The vast majority of non-Jews with an opinion believe that Jews: are usually hardworking people; have a strong faith in God; are warm and friendly people; and have contributed much to the cultural life of America.

Another means of putting the level of prejudice against Jews into perspective is to compare the social acceptance of Jews with that of other ethnic and racial groups. The current study indicates that the level of social acceptance of Jews is quite similar to that of Italian Americans. For example, 59 percent of non-Jews say they would not be bothered at all if their political party nominated a Jew for president compared to 62 percent of non-Italian Americans who say they would not be bothered at all by the nomination of an Italian American. In contrast, Black and Japanese Americans are considerably less likely than Jews or Italian Americans to be accepted as political candidates, neighbors, or potential marriage partners for one's children.

Consistently with the decline in traditional anti-Semitic stereotypes that has taken place since 1964, Jews have become more socially acceptable as marriage partners from the point of view of non-Jews. In 1964, just over one out of two (55 percent) non-Jews said they would be disturbed very little or not at all if their own child wanted to marry a Jew; today that figure is up to two out of three (66 percent).

The overall decline in anti-Semitism since 1964 is not primarily the result of changes in the views of individuals; rather it is the result of generational change. In 1964, older adults tended to be highly anti-Semitic. Their dying and replacement by today's young adults has resulted in lower levels of anti-Semitism, since young people today tend to be relatively unprejudiced. For example, 16 percent of 18 to 29 year olds are prejudiced compared to 31 percent of those 55 and over. It is the changing of generations, then, and not the changing of individual attitudes that is primarily responsible for a decline in anti-Semitism.

Increased tolerance of diversity is an important factor in declining anti-Semitism. This is related to the generational change. Since 1964, Americans have been led by young adults to an increasing tolerance of a variety of life-styles and beliefs. They are more willing to accept, for example, men with beards, the rights of atheists, and foreigners. This general tolerance for diversity is strongly tied to tolerance of Jews in particular—indicating that the increasing acceptance of Jews is, in part, a reflection of the more general trend toward increasing acceptance of social pluralism.

Other major societal trends, such as increased political conservatism and growing economic and energy concerns, do not appear to have had a major impact on anti-Semitism. In fact, individuals who have grown more conservative or who are quite concerned about economic or energy problems are not more likely to be anti-Semitic.

Christian fundamentalism is not a major factor in anti-Semitic beliefs. Christian fundamentalists have gained visibility and political power on the national level in recent years. However, the current study indicates that traditional religious beliefs have declined in prevalence since 1964. Despite this decline, Christian fundamentalists are somewhat more likely to be prejudiced against Jews than nonfundamentalists (25 percent of the Christian fundamentalists are prejudiced versus 18 percent of the nonfundamentalists). However, this higher level is due not to the direct effect of religious beliefs but to the fact that these people are older, less likely to be educated, and more likely to be nonwhite—all factors that are associated with anti-Semitic prejudice.

Social contact between Jews and non-Jews has both positive and negative sides. Among whites, social contact between Jews and non-Jews is associated with somewhat lower levels of anti-Semitism. For example, among those individuals who are prejudiced, 40 percent have a high level of social contact with Jews compared to 54 percent of the unprejudiced who have a high level of social contact with Jews.

What is perhaps more interesting than the overall relationship between higher levels of social contact and lower levels of anti-Semitism is the fact that among blacks the relationship is reversed. That is, among Black Americans, higher levels of contact with Jews are associated with higher levels of prejudice. The results of the study indicate that it is not black-Jewish contact per se that increases tensions, but rather the nature of that contact. Compared to white-Jewish contact, it is less likely to be based on friendship or informal social relations and more likely to take the form of economic contact.

Despite the significant decline in traditional anti-Semitic stereotypes, the belief in the perceived power of Jews and the perceived loyalty of Jews to Israel has become somewhat more widespread. While the overall decline in anti-Semitism covers a broad range of negative beliefs about Jews, it is not universal. Since 1964 Jews are increasingly likely to be viewed as more loyal to Israel than to the United States and as having too much power. In 1964, one out of ten (13 percent) non-Jews believed Jews have too much power in the United States; today that figure is up to one in five (23 percent).

Similarly, in 1964, four out of ten (39 percent) non-Jews believed Jews are more loyal to Israel than to the United States; today that figure has risen to nearly one out of two (48 percent). (These percentages are based on those with an opinion. See Table 3.1 for percentages based on total.)

American attitudes toward Israel have not had a negative impact on attitudes toward Jews. Attitudes toward Israel and attitudes toward American Jews are highly related. Individuals who are highly favorable in their outlook regarding Israel are less likely to be anti-Semitic. Those who are critical of Israel are more likely to be anti-Semitic. However, support for Israel is quite widespread among Americans and consequently attitudes toward Israel have not adversely affected attitudes toward American Jews. Nevertheless, if attitudes toward Israel became much more critical, it is possible that this could have a significant negative effect on American attitudes toward Jews.

Not surprisingly, American Jews are much more sensitive to both the presence and the potential of anti-Semitism in the United States. Jews are more likely to say they are aware of anti-Semitic incidents than non-Jews. They are also more likely to believe anti-Semitic incidents are on the rise and that a resurgence of anti-Semitism is possible.

Consistent with the differing views of Jews and non-Jews regarding anti-Semitic incidents is the fact that Jewish perceptions about the level of anti-Semitic beliefs are sharply at odds with the views actually expressed by non-Jews. For example most (76 percent) Jews believe that the majority of non-Jews believe that "Jews have too much power in the business world." Among non-Jews, one out of three (32 percent) actually expresses this belief.

NOTES

1. New York *Times*, October 9, 1980.
2. See discussion of limits of analysis of field studies and analysis of records, Chapter 2.
3. D. Yankelovich, *New Rules* (New York: Simon & Schuster, 1981), pp. 87–88.
4. See Chapter 6, note 1, for sources documenting increasing tolerance of diversity.
5. See H. Quinley and C. Glock. *Anti-Semitism in America* (New York: Free Press, 1979), pp. 11–12.

6. There are a number of published and unpublished analyses of trends in poll items on attitudes toward Jews in the United States including: C. H. Stember et al., *Jews in the Mind of America*; W. Schneider, "Anti-Semitism and Israel: A Report on American Public Opinion," December 1978, mimeographed; Louis Harris and Associates, "A Study of Attitudes toward Racial and Religious Minorities toward Women," 1978; New York *Times*, "Feelings toward Jews Found More Favorable in a Survey by Gallup," April 17, 1981. However, all of these reports are based on analysis of a relatively small number of trend items, and all but the Harris study are secondary analyses of existing data.

7. G. Selznick and S. Steinberg, *The Tenacity of Prejudice* (New York: Harper & Row, 1969).

8. Many early studies of anti-Semitism were conducted on quite limited samples. For example, T. W. Adorno et al., *The Authoritarian Personality*, while in many ways a pathbreaking survey of anti-Semitism, was based primarily on a sample of the Bay area in San Francisco. Perhaps the most comprehensive research program on anti-Semitism was The University of California Research Program on the Pattern of American Prejudice sponsored by the Anti-Defamation League of B'nai B'rith during the 1960s and 1970s. The results were published in seven volumes including: G. Selznick and S. Steinberg, *The Tenacity of Prejudice: Anti-Semitism in Contemporary America* (New York: Harper & Row, 1969); G. Marx, *Protest and Prejudice: A Study of Belief in the Black Community* (New York: Harper & Row, 1967); S. Lipset and E. Raab, *The Politics of Unreason: Right Wing Extremism in America 1890–1970* (New York: Harper & Row, 1970); C. Glock and R. Stark, *Christian Beliefs and Anti-Semitism* (New York: Harper & Row, 1966); R. Stark, B. Foster, C. Glock, and H. Quinley, *Wayward Shepherds: Prejudice and the Protestant Clergy* (New York: Harper & Row, 1971); C. Glock, R. Wuthnox, J. Piliavin, and M. Spencer, *Adolescent Prejudice* (New York: Harper & Row, 1975); C. Glock, G. Selznick, and J. Spaeth, *The Apathetic Majority: A Study Based on Public Responses to the Eichmann Trial* (New York: Harper & Row, 1966).

9. See Chapter 4 for a fuller discussion of the breakdown of the proportion of prejudiced and unprejudiced.

2

METHODOLOGICAL ISSUES IN THE
STUDY OF ANTI-SEMITISM

The focus of most of the sociological research on anti-Semitism in the United States has been the study of attitudes toward Jews and their determinants. The study of anti-Semitic attitudes raises two fundamental questions that must be addressed at the outset. Firstly, why study anti-Semitic attitudes when what is of greater concern is anti-Semitic behavior? Secondly, are the attitudes expressed in a survey a reliable indication of how people truly feel, or are they simply a reflection of what is socially acceptable?

WHY STUDY ANTI-SEMITIC ATTITUDES?

Survey research is not, of course, the only possible approach to studying the problem. Many other approaches exist, including field studies of communities or institutions (for example, a high school) where anti-Semitism is a reality, content analyses of popular periodicals or the documents or publications of hate groups, study of records of anti-Semitic incidents—noting, for example, the perpetrators and the characteristics of the communities. Despite these and other alternatives, the analysis of survey data has a number of advantages that are difficult or impossible to achieve through other approaches. The most important are representativeness, generalizability, known reliability, and the use of statistical analysis and statistical control.

Representativeness

One of the critical advantages of the sample survey is, of course, that it permits us to obtain a representative sampling of the views of members of a known universe in a way that is not ordinarily possible in field studies and case histories. Also, while content analysis can readily be based on representative samples of periodicals or other documents, these are samples of published opinion rather than the private opinions of a cross-section of ordinary individuals.

Generalizability

The importance of having a representative sampling of opinion is, of course, that it allows us to make generalizations about a known universe. In the current instance we are, for example, able to generalize about the beliefs of all non-Jews in the United States. Such generalizability is often quite limited when other methods of data gathering are used. For example, content analysis of public documents is limited in its generalizations to statements about the public pronouncements of a tiny minority of the population. Case histories of communities or institutions such as schools are limited to the community under study.

Known Reliability

Methods of analyzing the reliability of survey measurements have been developed over many years. The calculation of these reliability coefficients is relatively simple.[1] In contrast, the reliability of observations of someone doing a community study is much more difficult to assess. Similarly, the reliability of records or reports of anti-Semitic incidents are also difficult to assess for many of the same reasons that arrest records are notoriously unreliable measures of criminal activity.

Statistical Analysis and Statistical Control

Another advantage of the survey research approach is that it permits a degree of statistical analysis and statistical control that is generally not possible with most other approaches to data gathering, apart from experiments. The use of statistical analysis allows us to examine complex relationships that would not ordinarily be subject to analysis in field studies of anti-Semitism. For example, in the current study we are able to examine the relationship between religious orthodoxy and anti-Semitic beliefs controlling for age, education, and race. This access to statistical analysis permits a degree of control in survey research that is generally greater than most nonexperimental research designs.

THE ATTITUDE VERSUS BEHAVIOR ISSUE

While survey research has many advantages to recommend it, it does also have a number of problems. One of the central issues is the relationship between attitudes and behavior.

For nearly 50 years, social scientists have been concerned about this relationship.[2] Many analysts have argued the importance of situational elements in explaining the consistency or inconsistency of attitudes and behavior. The importance of knowledge of the situational elements of action is familiar to students of the history of anti-Semitism who know too well that anti-Semitic attitudes are endemic to Western culture but are ignited by particular events and circumstances.

It is essential that we understand the backdrop of attitudes and what supports them before we can hope to understand what ignites these negative feelings into anti-Semitic action. For how can we hope to understand what causes isolated anti-Semitic incidents or the emergence of institutionalized anti-Semitism without understanding the distribution of anti-Semitic beliefs and the factors that underlie them? There are at least three more specific reasons that make the study of anti-Semitic attitudes essential. First, attitudes toward Jews and other minorities tell us something important about the views and values of a culture. Studying changes in attitudes is therefore one means of studying cultural change in general. Second, anti-Semitic attitudes and behavior are linked. For example, in the current survey attitudes toward Jews are associated with social contact with Jews. While behavior may not be determined solely by attitudes, the latter serve as important barriers or inducements to behavioral change and therefore merit close scrutiny. Third, the study of the distribution of anti-Semitic attitudes on a nationally representative basis allows us to get a clearer understanding of the structural factors in American society that are responsible for prejudice in a way that is not possible using other approaches.

For example, the current study indicates that age is positively related to anti-Semitism—the older someone is, the more likely he or she is to be anti-Semitic; the lower the age (down to 18 years of age) the less likely he or she is to be anti-Semitic. In contrast, analyses of anti-Semitic incidents around the nation almost inevitably yield the conclusion that they are disproportionately carried out by teenagers. What are we to make of this apparent discrepancy in findings? Is anti-Semitism higher among the young or is it lower? Our own judgement on this question is that the disproportionate share of anti-Semitic incidents that are carried out by teenagers is a reflection of the fact that vandalism, in general, is more likely to be committed by teenagers[3] —rather than any special predilection of teenagers for anti-Semitism. The important point here is, again, that the survey research approach allows us to obtain generalizable findings about a known universe—something that is often quite difficult using other means of analysis.

THE SOCIAL DESIRABILITY ISSUE

Perhaps the most frequent methodological criticism directed against survey research on such sensitive issues as anti-Semitism is, How can you be sure that people are telling you the truth? Aren't people just going to give you socially acceptable answers? This is commonly referred to in the methodological literature as the problem of social desirability. In the current study the problem is compounded by the fact that many of the findings are based on a trend analysis, which raises the additional problem of a possible change in the social desirability of anti-Semitic beliefs since 1964. Three distinct findings serve to help undermine these arguments and concerns and support the soundness of the measures used in the study.

First, there is a high degree of reliability to the measure of anti-Semitism used in the current study—that is, the 11 items in the anti-Semitism index are highly correlated with one another. Therefore, a respondent who wanted to conceal anti-Semitic feelings would have to be consistent across a variety of measures.

Second, while most of the measures of anti-Semitism show a decline in negative attitudes since 1964, not all of the negative images of Jews have become less common. Indeed, belief in excessive Jewish loyalty to Israel has risen since 1964, an observation that is quite believable given the increasing visibility of the Middle East and the greater salience of Israel for most Americans.

Third, and perhaps most important, is the fact that the mean level of anti-Semitism among the cohort of Americans who were 18 to 55 in 1964 and are 35 years and over today has remained essentially the same. This stability over the 17-year period supports the idea that the social desirability of negative images of Jews has not changed dramatically since 1964. If the expression of anti-Semitic beliefs had become significantly more or less socially desirable since 1964, it is highly unlikely that the mean level of anti-Semitism in this cohort would have remained so stable after 17 years.

THE METHOD

The study was conducted in two phases. After an initial review of the literature, the first phase consisted of 50 depth interviews with Jews and non-Jews in all four regions of the nation. These had two objectives: to generate hypotheses for testing in the second, quantitative phase; and to help refine the quantitative questionnaire.

The second phase of the study was a national quantitative survey, the results of which are reported in this volume. The survey was based on a total of 1,215 personal interviews, representing all adults (18 years of age and over) in the contiguous United States. This sample consisted of a cross-sectional sample of 1,072 interviews and a supplemental sample of an additional 143 interviews with Jews and blacks. In all, 174 interviews were conducted with Jews and 127 with blacks. All interviewing on the current study took place between January 28, 1981 and March 6, 1981.

Another important aspect of the current study was the process of index conduction. Details of the respective indexes are discussed in the chapters in which they are introduced. For a more detailed discussion of the indexes see Appendixes B and C.

THE ANALYSIS

Knowing the proportion of Americans who accept an anti-Semitic belief is an important, yet limited finding. Once we know that 20 percent of non-Jews believe that "Jews have too much power in the United States," many new questions arise: Is that a lot or a little? Is the number on the rise or declining? How do different groups, such as men and women, feel?

In order to answer these and other questions, the current analysis (chapters 3 and 4) provides four distinct ways of looking at the level of anti-Semitism in contemporary U.S. society. First we examine the absolute level of anti-Semitic beliefs in the United States by exploring the proportion of Americans who accept or reject stereotypes about Jews. The second perspective we bring to bear is an analysis of the trends in attitudes toward Jews since 1964. The third is provided by comparing attitudes toward Jews with attitudes toward other ethnic and racial groups in the United States. The fourth and final perspective is an analysis of the extent of anti-Semitism among a broad range of demographic and social groups.

We then turn to an analysis of the factors that are associated with anti-Semitism (chapters 5 through 9). Next we examine the attitudes, beliefs, and experiences of Jews and non-Jews particularly as they relate to the perception and experience of anti-Semitic incidents (chapters 10 and 11). We conclude with an analysis of the major factors associated with anti-Semitism in the 1980s.

NOTES

1. See D. Magnusson, *Test Theory* (Reading, Mass.: Addison-Wesley, 1966).

2. R. T. La Pierre, "Attitudes Versus Actions," *Social Forces* 13 (1934): 230–237; A. Wicker, "Attitudes versus Actions: The Relationships of Verbal and Overt Behavioral Responses to Attitudes Objects," *Journal of Social Issues* 25 (1969): 25; M. Fishbein, "The Relationships Between Beliefs, Attitudes and Behavior," in *Cognitive Consistency*, ed. S. Feldman, (New York: Academic Press, 1966); L. Kahle, D. Klingel, and R. Kulka, "A Longitudinal Study of Adolescents' Attitude Behavior Consistency," *Public Opinion Quarterly*, Fall, 1981, pp. 402–414.

3. "Uniform Crime Reports—1968/U.S. Department of Justice," in *Crime and Justice*, vol. I, L. Radzinowicz and M. E. Wolfgang, eds. (New York: Basic Books, 1971), p. 161.

3

BELIEFS ABOUT AMERICAN JEWS

Much of the research on public attitudes toward Jews has been prompted by exposure to anti-Semitic incidents. For example, *The Authoritarian Personality* and *Dynamics of Prejudice* were sponsored by the American Jewish Committee in the mid and late forties as a means of more fully understanding the Holocaust.[1] "How could it be," they asked, "that in a culture of law, order, and reason, there should have survived the irrational remnants of ancient racial and religious hatreds?"[2]

The five-year study of anti-Semitism sponsored by the Anti-Defamation League and conducted by the Survey Research Center of the University of California at Berkeley during the 1960s was prompted by a spate of anti-Semitic incidents that followed the desecration of a Cologne synagogue on Christmas Day, 1959. Indeed the current effort was itself prompted, in part, by concern about the outbreak of anti-Semitic incidents that followed the bombing of the rue Copernic synagogue in Paris in 1980.

Given the circumstances that have prompted the major efforts to research attitudes toward Jews in the United States, it should come as no surprise that most of this research has focused on negative images. For each study was, in its own way, an attempt to understand the environment that produced anti-Semitic attitudes and behavior.

POSITIVE AND NEGATIVE IMAGES OF JEWS

We begin our analysis of the survey results with a discussion of the positive and negative images of Jews held by non-Jews. It is important to note that the evaluation of whether a belief was to be considered positive or negative was not based upon the judgement of the researchers. Rather, an image was viewed as positive if it was associated with other positive images and as negative if it was associated with other negative images. For example, the belief that Jews have a strong faith in God was associated with positive images and consequently was viewed as such. The view that "Jews have more money than most people" was associated with negative characteristics and was therefore viewed as a negative.

Despite the focus on negative images in much of the previous research it is clear that, generally speaking, positive images of Jews are more pervasive than negative ones. A substantial majority of non-Jews believe that Jews are: usually hard-working people (81 percent); have a strong faith in God (71 percent); are warm and friendly people (64 percent); and are just as honest as other businessmen (60 percent). Also, one out of two (53 percent) non-Jews feel that Jews have contributed much to the cultural life of America. No single negative image of Jews approaches these positive sentiments in terms of its level of acceptance. The most widespread negative belief about Jews is that they "stick together too much," a stereotype that is accepted by 40 percent of non-Jews and rejected by 35 percent.

One interesting dimension to attitudes about Jews is that while positive and negative beliefs are negatively correlated, the correlations tend to be quite small. So, for example, the negative correlation between the belief that Jews "stick together too much" (presumably to the exclusion of non-Jews) and the belief that Jews are "warm and friendly" is quite low ($r = -.11$).[3] That is, non-Jews who believe that Jews are warm and friendly are only slightly less likely to believe that "Jews stick together too much." This generally low negative correlation between the negative stereotype and positive stereotypes is also reflected in the fact that the positive images constitute a separate factor (see factor analysis in Appendix C) in a factor analysis of images of Jews.

Implicit in the low negative correlation between the positive and negative images of Jews is the fact that it is quite possible for individuals to hold both positive and negative images. Acceptance of

Table 3.1. Beliefs about Jews among Non-Jews

	Probably true (%)	Probably false (%)	Not sure (%)
Jews are usually hard working people.	81	6	13
Jews have a strong faith in God.	71	8	21
Jews are warm and friendly people.	64	10	26
Jews are just as honest as other businessmen.	60	17	23
Jews have contributed much to the cultural life of America.	53	14	33
Jews stick together too much.	40	35	25
Jews always like to be at the head of things.	38	35	27
Jewish employers go out of their way to hire Jews.	37	28	35
Jews have too much power in the business world.[a]	32	55	13
Jews are stubborn and resist change.	30	30	40
Jews are more loyal to Israel than to America.	30	32	38
Jews should stop complaining about what happened to them in Nazi Germany.	28	42	30
International banking is pretty much controlled by Jews.	21	28	51
The movie and television industries are pretty much controlled by Jews.	25	29	46
Jews are liberal politically.	25	18	57
Jews are more willing to use shady practices.	23	46	31
The trouble with Jewish businessmen is that they are so shrewd and tricky.	20	54	26
Jews have too much power in the United States.[a]	20	67	13
Jews have a lot of irritating faults.	19	48	33
Jews don't care what happens to anyone but their own kind.	16	59	25
Jews are always stirring up trouble with their ideas.	10	61	29
Jews today are trying to push in where they are not wanted.	16	70	14

[a]These statements were posed as questions designed to elicit "yes," "no," or "don't know" responses.

positive images of Jews is by no means a guarantee against anti-Semitism. Indeed, despite the widespread positive images of Jews, acceptance of certain traditional anti-Semitic beliefs also remains quite widespread. For example, one in five (21 percent) non-Jews and more than four out of ten (43 percent) of those with an opinion believe that "international banking is pretty much controlled by Jews." Similarly, 39 percent of non-Jews and nearly one out of two (48 percent) of those with an opinion believe that "Jews are more loyal to Israel than to America." Clearly, then, anti-Semitism remains a serious social problem in contemporary U.S. society. Perhaps one of the most important questions we can ask about anti-Semitism is whether it is on the rise or on the decline. This is the issue to which we now turn.

TRENDS IN BELIEFS ABOUT JEWS

Using *The Tenacity of Prejudice* as a baseline, the following are the major trends in beliefs about Jews that have emerged between 1964 and 1981.

The Image of Jews as Unethical: Declining

As minorities in Christian nations, Jews have for centuries been subject to attack for being unethical. For 400 years, the figure of Shylock has stood as a symbol of the unethical Jew who follows the letter of the law beyond the bounds of justice and decency.

According to the current survey, one of the most consistent and dramatic changes in the image of Jews in recent years is the decline in the view that they are unethical. Compared to 1964, non-Jews are less likely to view Jewish businessmen as dishonest, shrewd, or tricky; and are also less likely to believe in general that Jews are more willing than others to use shady business practices to get what they want (48 percent) with an opinion agreed in 1964 versus 33 percent with an opinion in 1981).

The Image of Jews as Clannish: No Real Change

By the very act of maintaining their separateness as a social group, Jews are subject to the charge of clannishness. Though it has been

Table 3.2. Trends in Negative Beliefs about Jews among Non-Jews

	1964 (%)	1981 (%)	Net difference: 1981–1964 (%)
Probably true			
[a]The movie and television industries are pretty much controlled by Jews.	70	46	−24
[a]Jews have a lot of irritating faults.	48	29	−19
[a]Jews are more willing than others to use shady practices to get what they want.	48	33	−15
[a]The trouble with Jewish businessmen is that they are so shrewd and tricky that other people don't have a fair chance in competition.	40	27	−13
[a]Jews are just as honest as other businessmen.	34	22	−12
[a]International banking is pretty much controlled by Jews.	55	43	−12
[a]Jews always like to be at the head of things.	63	52	−11
Jews should stop complaining about what happened to them in Nazi Germany.	51	40	−10
[a]Jews don't care what happens to anyone but their own kind.	30	22	−8
[a]Jews stick together too much.	58	53	−5
Jewish employers go out of their way to hire other Jews.	60	57	−3
Jews today are trying to push in where they are not wanted.	21	19	−2
Jews are always stirring up trouble with their ideas.	13	14	+1
[a]Jews have too much power in the business world.[b]	33	37	+4
[a]Jews are more loyal to Israel than to America.	39	48	+9
[a]Jews have too much power in the United States.[b]	13	23	+10

[a]11-item anti-Semitism index.

[b]These statements were posed as questions designed to elicit "yes," "no," or "don't know" responses.

Note: Based on those with an opinion.

Table 3.3. Trends in Beliefs about Jews among Non-Jews

	Total			1964 Cohort		
				1964	1981	
					35	
	1964 (%)	1981 (%)	Net difference 1981–1964 (%)	18–54 Years of age (%)	Years or more (%)	Net difference: 1981–1964 (%)
Probably true[a]						
Too much power in United States	13	23	+10	9	27	+18
Care only about own kind	30	21	−9	25	23	−2
Not as honest as other businessmen	30	22	−8	28	21	−7
Too much power in business world	33	37	+4	28	41	+13
More loyal to Israel than to United States	39	48	+9	32	49	+17
Control international banking	55	43	−12	44	51	+7
Shrewd and tricky in business	40	27	−13	33	29	−4
Have a lot of irritating faults	48	28	−20	44	32	−12
Use shady practices to get ahead	48	33	−15	43	37	−6
Stick together too much	58	53	−5	54	59	+5
Always like to head things	63	52	−11	59	55	−4
Mean level of anti-Semitism	41.5	35.1		36.2	38.5	

[a]Items used in anti-Semitism index.
Note: Based on those with an opinion.

eroded slightly, the image of clannishness endures as, perhaps, the most common negative stereotype about Jews. A majority of non-Jews with an opinion continue to accept the views that "Jews stick together too much" (53 percent) and that "Jewish employers go out of their way to hire other Jews" (57 percent).

Jewish Control of Business and Industry: Declining, but Still a Problem

Another stereotype that has declined sharply since 1964 is the belief that Jews control international banking and the movie and television industry. However, while the decline has been sharp, beliefs about Jewish power in business and industry continue to be fairly widespread. For example, more than one out of five (28 percent) non-Jews and four out of ten (43 percent) non-Jews with an opinion believe that Jews control international banking.

Offensive Personal Qualities: Declining

Since 1964, there has also been a drop in the proportion of non-Jews who accept stereotypic beliefs about the offensive personal qualities of Jews. Today, for example, just over one in four (29 percent) non-Jews with an opinion say that "Jews have a lot of irritating faults" compared to nearly one out of two (48 percent) in 1964. Similarly, 22 percent with an opinion now feel "Jews don't care what happens to anyone but their own kind" compared to 30 percent in 1964.

The Perceived Power of Jews: Up Slightly

In 1964, one in ten (13 percent) non-Jews with an opinion believed that Jews had too much power in the United States. That figure has now risen to nearly one in four (23 percent). This belief has been quite variable over time, rising and falling in response to the events of the day. Perhaps most important is the fact that while the perception of Jewish power is somewhat higher today than in the mid-1960s, it has not returned to the high levels recorded by Gallup in the 1940s and 1950s.[4]

Israel and the Dual Loyalty Issue: Up Slightly

Related to the image of Jews as clannish is the issue of whether American Jews are more loyal to Israel than to the United States. The dual loyalty issue is another area where attitudes toward Jews have changed since the mid-1960s. In 1964, four out of ten (39 percent) non-Jews with an opinion agreed that "Jews are more loyal to Israel than to America"; by 1981 that figure had risen to one out of two (48 percent).

Without panel data to link a change in one attitude with a change in another, it is not possible to relate the perceived increase in Jewish power with the issue of Jews' perceived loyalty to Israel. However, it seems likely that these two trends are linked. Indeed, complaints about the influence of Israel and "the Jewish lobby" on U.S. foreign policy are not uncommon and may be at the heart of both trends.

Attitudes toward the Holocaust: More Sympathetic

In their book, *The New Anti-Semitism*, Forster and Epstein argue that there is widespread concern in the American Jewish community over the future of the position of Jews in America. "In short, the Jewish people, a scant three decades after the annihilation of fully a third of its ranks, is affected with a profound uneasiness. Is the pendulum swinging back? Is there a new anti-Semitism? Is the old vinegar in new casks out of different vineyards? Has moral outrage become moral indifference?"[5] The gist of their argument is that, while the Holocaust produced a sense of moral outrage around the world that resulted in major gains in the status of Jews and other minorities, the passage of years has brought a growing indifference to the concerns of Jews in the United States. Because of this growing indifference to anti-Semitism among a broad range of Americans, they argue, hostility toward Jews has been able to grow among the radical left, radical right, pro-Arab groups, and black extremists.

While Forster and Epstein's hypothesis about the declining moral outrage about the Holocaust may have some validity as far as extremist groups are concerned, when it comes to the average American, there is little evidence to support their premise that the Holocaust produced an increase in acceptance of Jews in the United States. Indeed, as Stember has pointed out, the postwar polls conducted in the United States show little evidence that the Holocaust had any effect on American attitudes toward Jews.

> The appalling suffering of European Jewry under Hitler, as well as the wholehearted identification of Jews everywhere with the Allied cause, might be thought to have made Americans more sympathetic toward their Jewish fellow citizens. The results of opinion polls make it clear that no such change took place. In two surveys, both dating back from 1945, over three-quarters of all respondents said the mass killings in Europe had not affected their own attitudes toward Jews in America.[6]

The findings of our own study also support the idea that Forster and Epstein are wrong if they believe popular moral outrage was widespread after the war and has declined since. Indeed, despite the passage of time, Americans today are less likely to believe that "Jews should stop complaining about what happened to them in Nazi Germany." In 1964, with the Holocaust only sixteen years behind them, the majority (51 percent) of Americans with an opinion agreed with this anti-Semitic sentiment. By 1981, that figure had declined to 40 percent. Among young people who were not born by the end of the war only 38 percent agree. Clearly, the memory of moral outrage about the Holocaust does not appear to be a major factor in explaining anti-Semitism or indifference to it.

Declining Anti-Semitism: Generational, Not Individual, Change

Changes in national attitudes over time can come from several sources: changes in the views of individuals, changes in the composition of society, or both. The overall decline in anti-Semitism that has occurred in the United States since 1964 is not primarily the result of changes in attitudes of individuals; rather, it is the result of societal change.

An examination of the views of that cohort of Americans who were adults in 1964 and are likely to be alive today (18 to 55 years of age in 1964 and 35 years of age and over in 1981) reveals that among these individuals there has been no overall decline in anti-Semitism.

In 1964, the mean level of anti-Semitism (based on those with an opinion) was 36.2. In 1981, in this same age cohort (now 35 years of age and over), it was 38.5, indicating that there had been essentially no change after a period of nearly 20 years. What has changed in this age cohort was not the overall level of anti-Semitism but the nature of anti-Semitic belief. Members of this age cohort were less likely in 1981 as compared to 1964 to hold stereotypic views about the negative personal qualities of Jews. However, they were more likely to accept the idea of excessive Jewish power and loyalty to Israel. We see, therefore, that there is some justification for Forster and Epstein's concern about "the new anti-Semitism."

Nevertheless, the general level of anti-Semitism has indeed declined in the United States. This has not, however, been the result of changes in the views of those individuals who were adults in 1964. Rather, it is the result of two societal factors: 1. the death of many of those individuals who were 55 years of age and over in 1964 (and who were highly anti-Semitic) and 2. the coming of age of those individuals who were young children in the mid-1960s and are 18 to 34 years of age today (and who are highly tolerant).

The decline in anti-Semitism that we have noted has not come about as the result of changes in the attitudes of individuals. Indeed, those Americans who were adults in 1964 and are likely to be alive today have remained remarkably stable in their overall level of anti-Semitic beliefs. The decline has come about because of a new generation of Americans who are better educated, have more contact with Jews, and are generally more tolerant of diversity of all kinds—issues that we will be returning to in subsequent chapters.

THE IMPLICATION OF THE COHORT FINDING

While the finding that the overall decline in anti-Semitism is the result of generational change may be less morally satisfying than uncovering a change of heart on an individual level, it is, in other ways, more reassuring.

The fact that the mean level of anti-Semitism in the cohort born between 1910 and 1946 has remained essentially unchanged supports the view that the general decline is real and is not simply an artifact of a change in the social acceptability of the questionnaire items. The stability of attitudes in this cohort supports the validity of the overall decline because it indicates that the social acceptability of espousing anti-Semitic beliefs has not changed substantially in the culture as a whole.

Perhaps even more important than this methodological concern is the fact that a number of features of today's social and demographic environment provide us with reason to believe that the level of anti-Semitism may continue to decline in the future as the current generation of younger and better-educated Americans continues to "displace" an older, more anti-Semitic generation.

First, as has already been pointed out, the overall level of negative attitudes toward Jews has been quite stable since 1964 in that cohort of non-Jews born between 1910 and 1946. The fact that the level of anti-Semitic belief has remained stable despite the turmoil of the past two decades provides reason to believe that it will not rise in this group in the decades ahead.

Second, individuals born between 1947 and 1964 (today's 18 to 34 year olds) have significantly lower levels of anti-Semitic beliefs than older adults, in large part because of their higher levels of education and greater tolerance of diversity. This baby boom generation will play an increasingly significant role in U.S. society as they mature, and this large role should contribute to a further lowering of the overall level of anti-Semitism in American society as they move through the life cycle, continuing to displace older, more anti-Semitic adults.

Third, as the parents of today, the baby boom generation can be expected to raise a generation of children and young adults who are, like themselves, more tolerant of Jews and other minorities than were previous generations.

Fourth, education is a critical factor in declining anti-Semitism, and the educational attainment of the nation continues to rise. During the 1970s the proportion of Americans who did not complete high school dropped from 45 percent to 32 percent.[7] Even without any further increases in the educational attainment of young adults, the average level of education in the nation will continue to rise, as today's crop of young adults continues to replace an older, less educated population.

Our general assessment then, is that while the history of anti-Semitism provides us with reason to be skeptical about the "enlightenment" offered by education, there are sound reasons to believe that a higher level of education will continue to move further generations of Americans in the direction of increased tolerance for Jews and other minorities.

A COMPARISON OF ATTITUDES TOWARD MINORITIES

Comparisons with previous studies provide one point of reference. They permit the identification of the magnitude and direction of changes in attitudes. Trend analysis is a useful interpretative aid in that it gives a fuller meaning to the results of the current survey. Similarly, comparing attitudes toward Jews with those toward other groups allows us to get a clearer picture of the amount of prejudice against Jews relative to the amount of prejudice against other groups.

Three groups were chosen for comparative purposes: Black Americans, Japanese Americans, and Italian Americans. Black Americans were chosen because, despite recent gains, they remain among the least accepted groups in American society, and as such they are a benchmark against which the position of Jews can be compared. Italian Americans, on the other hand, were chosen because, despite their acceptance into the mainstream, they remain a recognizable ethnic group. Finally, Japanese Americans were chosen because the

Table 3.4. Beliefs about Minorities in the Total Non-Jewish
Sample Exclusive of the Members of the Group Being Described

	Group being asked about			
	Jews (%)	Italian Americans (%)	Black Americans (%)	Japanese Americans (%)
Believe group has too much power in the United States	23	14	17	9
Believe group has too much power in the business world	37	17	8	20
Believe group is very family oriented	95	93	56	92
Believe group tries to push in where they are not wanted	18	16	50	19
Believe group has more money than most people on average	62	16	4	21
Believe group is more ambitious than other people	52	18	6	42

Note: Based on those with an opinion.

image of the Japanese is in some ways quite similar to that of the Jews: hardworking, successful, and family oriented.

In relation to the images of Black Americans, Italian Americans, and Japanese Americans, that of Jews is a mixture of positive and negative elements. On the negative side is a constellation of beliefs relating to their perceived wealth, power, and influence in business and the professions. For example, Jews are more likely than other groups to be seen as having too much influence in business and banking, having more money than most people on average, and being more ambitious than other people.

Despite these potentially negative images of Jewish power and influence, in other ways the image of Jews is favorable. They are widely viewed as family oriented. They are viewed as less pushy than blacks and as no more so than Italian or Japanese Americans. While Jews are more likely to be seen as having too much influence in business and banking, they are not seen as particularly influential when it comes to government, politics, education, and a variety of other areas.

THE SOCIAL ACCEPTANCE OF JEWS

For more than 50 years,[8] researchers have been studying the level of social acceptance or social distance that exists between individuals and social groups. Consistently with the already noted decline in anti-Semitic beliefs, the current study indicates that the social acceptance of Jews has also increased since 1964. In particular, they have come to be seen as more socially acceptable as marriage partners from the point of view of non-Jews. In 1964, just over one out of two (55 percent) non-Jews said that they would be disturbed very little or not at all if their own child wanted to marry a Jew. Today, that figure is up to two out of three (66 percent). Also, few (6 percent) non-Jews say they would prefer *not* to have any Jewish neighbors and only one in five (21 percent) say they would be bothered by the nomination of a Jew for president by their own political party.

COMPARISON OF SOCIAL ACCEPTANCE

The current study indicates that the level of acceptance of American Jews is quite similar to that of Italian Americans and substantially

Table 3.5. Social Distance/Acceptance in the Total Sample
Exclusive of the Members of the Group Being Asked About

	Group being asked about			
	Jews (%)	Italian Americans (%)	Black Americans (%)	Japanese Americans (%)
Feelings about having a child marry a member of various groups				
Would object strongly	14	10	53	23
Would object somewhat	14	12	17	18
Would object a little	15	10	11	14
Would object not at all	51	62	37	37
Not sure	6	6	5	8
Feelings about having members of various groups in your neighborhood				
Would like to have some	5	6	5	4
Wouldn't make any difference	87	85	61	82
Prefer not to have any	6	6	31	10
Not sure	2	3	3	4
Feelings about having a member of various groups nominated for president by your political party				
Would be bothered very much	9	8	20	18
Would be bothered somewhat	12	10	15	15
Would be bothered very little	14	14	13	11
Would be bothered not at all	59	62	48	50
Not sure	6	6	4	6

greater than that of Japanese and Black Americans. For example, 66 percent of non-Jews say they would object a little or not at all if their child married a Jew, while 72 percent of non-Italians said they would object a little or not at all if their child married an Italian American. The comparable figure for Black Americans is 25 percent and for Japanese Americans 51 percent. The social acceptance of Jews and Italian Americans is also quite similar when it comes to political candidacy and contact with neighbors.

Overall then, the image of Jews and their level of social acceptance indicates that while prejudice against them continues, it is quite
limited in relation to that directed against nonwhite groups. And
again, the social acceptance of Jews is quite similar to that of Italian
Americans.

SUMMARY

Anti-Semitism has declined significantly in the United States
since the mid-1960s. This has been most evident when it comes to
traditional negative images of Jewish character such as those relating
to dishonesty, shrewdness, assertiveness, or willingness to use shady
business practices.

The decline is not the result of changes in the attitudes of individuals. Rather, it is the result of societal changes. An examination of
the views of that cohort of Americans who were adults in 1964 (18
to 55 years) and are alive today (35 years and over) reveals that there
has been no general decline in anti-Semitism. Thus, rather than being
the result of changes in the view of individuals, the overall decline in
anti-Semitic beliefs is the result of two societal factors: 1. the death
of many of those individuals who were 55 and over in 1964 (and
were highly anti-Semitic); and 2. the coming of age of those who
were young children in the mid-1960s and are 18 to 35 years old
today. Overall, then it is generational rather than individual change
that is responsible for declining anti-Semitism.

NOTES

1. T. W. Adorno, et al., *The Authoritarian Personality* (New York: W. W.
Norton, 1950); B. Bettelheim and M. Janowitz, *Dynamics of Prejudice: A Psychological and Sociological Study of Veterans* (New York: Harper, 1950).

2. Adorno, et al., p. v.

3. At several points in the analysis, we make use of correlation coefficients
and partial correlation coefficients. For the reader with no statistical training
some brief description of these is in order. A correlation coefficient is a measure
of association, which usually spans a continuum running from +1.0 to –1.0. A
correlation of +1.0 indicates a perfect positive correlation and means that an
increase in one variable (for example, education) is associated with an increase in
a second (for example, tolerance)—the more education, the more tolerance. A

correlation of −1.0 represents a perfect negative correlation and indicates that an increase in one variable (for example, education) is associated with a decrease in a second variable (for example, anti-Semitism)—the more education, the less anti-Semitism. A correlation of 0 indicates that two variables bear no relationship with one another.

A partial correlation is a measure of association between two variables (for example, age and anti-Semitism) after the effect of one or more additional variables has been statistically "removed." A partial correlation between age and anti-Semitism if we control for education would tell us the effect of age on anti-Semitism after "removing" the effects caused by the fact that younger people are better educated and better educated people are less anti-Semitic.

4. Gallup has tracked the perception of Jewish power since the 1940s using a question phrased somewhat differently: "Do you think the Jews are trying to get too much power in the U.S." In 1952, 33 percent agreed with this statement; in 1965, 12 percent agreed; in 1979 it had risen back to 22 percent.

5. A. Forster and B. Epstein, *The New Anti-Semitism* (New York: McGraw Hill, 1974), p. 3.

6. C. H. Stember et al., *Jews in the Mind of America* (New York: Basic Books, 1966), p. 142.

7. U.S. Chamber of Commerce, Statistical Abstract of the United States: 1980 (Washington, D.C.: Government Printing Office, 1980).

8. E. S. Bogardus, *Immigration and Race Attitudes* (Boston: D.C. Heath, 1928).

4

THE EXTENT OF ANTI-SEMITISM

One of the most common methodological devices in social science research is the use of a scale or index. In survey research, an index is a single summary measure created by combining the results of a number of separate questionnaire items.

The process of index construction presents the survey researcher with both problems and opportunities. The opportunity resides in having an analytical device that is descriptive of a complex concept with a degree of reliability that would not be possible using single item measures. On the negative side, constructing a descriptive index presents the researcher with a variety of problems. In addition to the traditional concerns about reliability and validity, the principal problem is reducing the arbitrariness in each step of the process: item selection, scoring, and the creation of cut-off points.

In order to provide such a single summary measure of anti-Semitism, the current study made use of the 11-item index of anti-Semitic beliefs developed at the University of California at Berkeley for *The Tenacity of Prejudice*. The results of the item analysis in the current study indicate that this measure minimizes the arbitrariness of index construction and is highly reliable.

The items used in the anti-Semitism index were as follows:[1]

too much power in U.S.;
care only about own kind;
not as honest as other businessmen;
too much power in business world;

more loyal to Israel than to America;
control international banking;
shrewd and tricky in business;
have a lot of irritating faults;
use shady practices to get ahead;
stick together too much;
always like to head things.

Using this index of anti-Semitism, we find that 45 percent of all non-Jews are unprejudiced—that is, relatively free of anti-Semitic beliefs; 23 percent are prejudiced, that is, accept a wide variety of stereotypes about Jews; and 32 percent are neutral, that is, neither

Figure 4.1. The Distribution of Anti-Semitism among Non-Jews

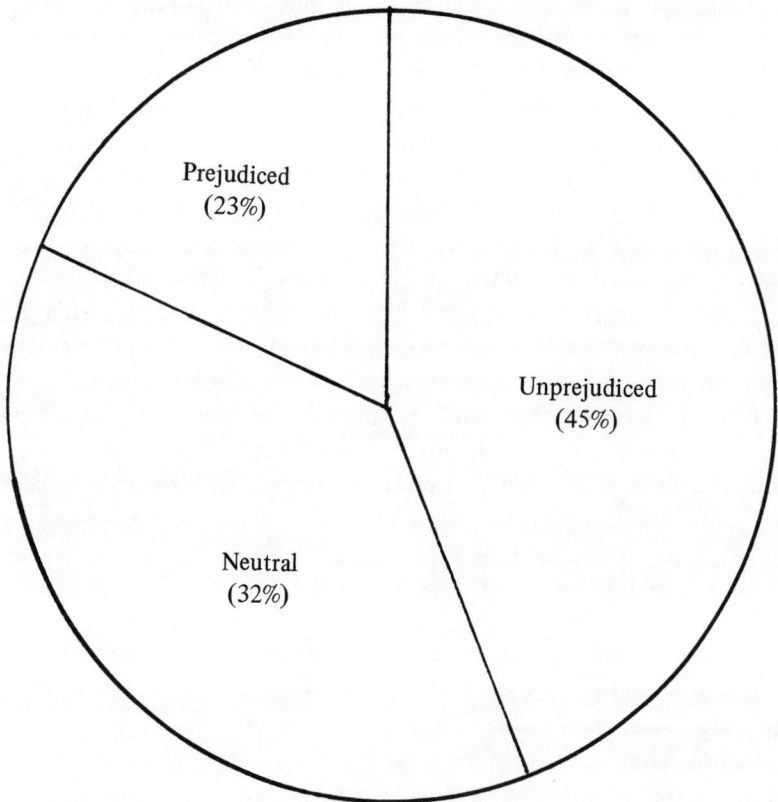

strongly prejudiced nor unprejudiced. Before turning to an analysis of the distribution of anti-Semitic beliefs in the population at large, we begin with a brief examination of the index itself.

THE STRUCTURE OF ANTI-SEMITIC BELIEFS

The items that were selected for consideration as possible elements of an index of anti-Semitism consisted of 24 negative beliefs about Jews. Included in this group were all 11 items from the Selznick and Steinberg (1964) index and 13 additional items suggested by the literature or by the pilot phase of the study. The first step in the creation of the index was a principal components factor analysis. This technique separates items into groupings (factors) that are relatively consistent internally and relatively distinct from one another. These factors can be thought of as the underlying dimensions that constitute a more simple structure of belief. Through an analysis of these distinctive factors of belief we are able to explore whether the structure of beliefs about Jews has changed since Selznick and Steinberg's study.

This analysis of the factor structure of beliefs is a critical step in interpretation since changes in the level of anti-Semitism noted in Chapter 3 could be, in part, the result of changes in the meaning of individual items. Such a change in meaning would be likely to be reflected in a change in their relationship to other items and would consequently produce a change in the factor structure.

The results of the factor analysis indicate that, generally speaking, the structure of anti-Semitic belief has changed little since 1964. Despite the introduction of a number of new items, the four-factor solution reveals essentially the same basic dimensions that were evident in 1964: traditional stereotypes about Jews; the power dimension; the positive image dimension; and the wealth ambition dimension. Indeed, even the factor loadings of individual items remains remarkably stable (see Appendix C for factor analysis).

Since the factor analysis of the 25 items measuring attitudes indicated that the factor structure of anti-Semitic beliefs had remained essentially unchanged since 1964, the 11-item index was again used in the current study. Apart from the value of continuity, the principal asset of the index is its high reliability (alpha = .81).[2]

THE SCORING PROCESS

The anti-Semitism index consists of three-point scales in the form of yes/no/not sure or true/false/not sure responses. The scoring process involved assigning the respondent one point for each anti-Semitic statement that was accepted. Selznick and Steinberg chose to define anti-Semitism as the presence of anti-Semitic beliefs without regard to whether the "absence" of anti-Semitic belief was due to taking a positive position or answering "not sure."

Our own analysis indicates that this scoring procedure and one that substitutes the mean score on an item for all "not sures" are of course, very highly correlated (r = .95). Also, not sure responses are, in good part, the result of low levels of contact with Jews.[3] Since the "not sure" response provides useful information about a respondent's views, it should be incorporated into the decision rules regarding how to characterize a respondent's level of anti-Semitism. These decision rules are explained in the next section.

THE CUT-OFF POINTS

The final sphere where the arbitrariness of the research process can intervene is in the selection of cut-off points. Setting the cut-off points at "high" or "low" levels has an impact on both the number of respondents at each level and the possible usefulness of the analytical category. In the current instance, the levels of anti-Semitism were set in a manner consistent with Selznick and Steinberg.[4]

Prejudiced—accept five or more anti-Semitic beliefs.

Neutral—accept four or fewer anti-Semitic beliefs and give not sure/ no answer response to four or more items.

Unprejudiced—accept four or fewer anti-Semitic beliefs and give not sure/no answer response to fewer than four items.

The appropriateness of this classification procedure is demonstrated by Table 4.1. A majority of those labelled as prejudiced accept almost all of the anti-Semitic beliefs while relatively few of those who are neutral or unprejudiced accept them. What distinguishes the neutrals is not merely their characteristically low level of acceptance of negative beliefs about Jews, but also the fact that they are less

Table 4.1. Cross Tabulation of Anti-Semitism Index and
Its Constituent Items among Non-Jews

	Total (%)	Anti-Semitism index		
		Prejudiced (%)	Neutral (%)	Unprejudiced (%)
Too much power in the United States	20	56	7	10
Care only about own kind	16	52	8	4
Not as honest as other businessmen	17	40	6	12
Too much power in the business world	32	67	18	23
More loyal to Israel than to United States	30	63	18	21
Control international banking	21	55	10	13
Shrewd and tricky in business	20	60	7	8
Have a lot of irritating faults	19	48	8	13
Use shady practices to get ahead	23	66	18	21
Stick together too much	40	76	26	33
Always like to head things	38	52	22	27

likely to accept positive images of Jews as well. For example, 69 percent of the unprejudiced believe that Jews have contributed much to the cultural life of the country compared to 54 percent of the prejudiced and 31 percent of the neutrals.

PROFILE

Having briefly discussed the underpinnings of the anti-Semitism index, let us now turn to a discussion of the distribution of anti-Semitism in various demographic groups. Prejudice against Jews is most likely to be found among non-Jews who are less educated, older (55 and over or retired), living in large cities, or black.

Individuals who are relatively free of anti-Semitic prejudice are more likely to be found among those who are better educated, pro-

Table 4.2. Profile of Anti-Semitism among Non-Jews

		Prejudiced (%)	Neutral (%)	Unprejudiced (%)
Total non-Jews	(100%)	23	32	45
Sex				
Men	(100%)	23	28	49
Women	(100%)	23	35	42
Race				
White	(100%)	21	30	49
Black	(100%)	37	41	22
Religion				
Catholic	(100%)	25	32	43
Total Protestant	(100%)	22	33	45
White Protestant	(100%)	21	32	47
Age				
18–29 years	(100%)	16	36	48
30–39 years	(100%)	23	26	51
40–54 years	(100%)	21	25	54
55 years and over	(100%)	31	37	32
Respondent's education				
Less than high school graduate	(100%)	28	38	34
High school graduate	(100%)	26	35	39
Some college	(100%)	16	23	61
College graduate/ postgraduate	(100%)	15	19	66
Respondent's occupation				
Professional/executive	(100%)	15	26	59

(Table continued on page 37.)

fessionals/executives, residents of the western states, or residents of middle-sized cities or suburbs.

Those whose attitudes toward Jews are neither particularly favorable nor unfavorable (neutral) are more likely to be found among blacks and in those parts of the country where there are relatively few Jews, including the South and small towns and rural areas.

Overall then, there are a large number of demographic factors that are associated with anti-Semitic beliefs. Several of these, such as age and education, are themselves highly correlated. In order to disentangle the separate effects of these many demographic factors,

Table 4.2, continued

		Prejudiced (%)	Neutral (%)	Unprejudiced (%)
Other white-collar	(100%)	29	19	52
Blue-collar	(100%)	21	37	42
Retired	(100%)	37	38	25
Housewife	(100%)	23	37	40
Region				
Northeast	(100%)	25	25	50
Midwest	(100%)	26	29	45
South	(100%)	23	41	36
West	(100%)	17	24	59
Where raised				
Large city	(100%)	35	19	46
Medium-size city	(100%)	19	30	51
Suburb of a large city	(100%)	17	27	56
Small town	(100%)	19	34	47
Farm/rural area	(100%)	28	42	30
City size				
1,000,000 or more	(100%)	45	8	47
500,000–999,999	(100%)	20	39	41
250,000–499,999	(100%)	17	34	49
100,000–249,999	(100%)	26	32	42
50,000–99,999	(100%)	9	23	68
10,000–49,999	(100%)	25	26	49
Under 10,000/rural unincorporated suburban	(100%)	20	41	39

partial correlation and multiple regression analyses were performed. The results of a stepwise linear regression indicate that there are three demographic factors with significant independent explanatory power. These are the respondent's educational level, age, and race. After controlling for these three, we find that other demographic characteristics add little or nothing to our ability to explain the variation in anti-Semitic beliefs. For example, after controlling for age, education, and race, we find that the partial correlation between anti-Semitism and father's education, mother's education, and total family income all drop to .05 or below.

Because of the significance of these three factors, we turn now to a fuller discussion of the impact of education, age, and race on anti-Semitic beliefs.

ANTI-SEMITISM AND EDUCATION

Education is clearly the most powerful demographic correlate of anti-Semitic beliefs. Individuals who are highly educated are significantly less likely to be anti-Semitic. Among non-Jews with less than a high school diploma, 28 percent are prejudiced and 33 percent are unprejudiced. Among those who are college graduates, 14 percent are prejudiced and 61 percent are unprejudiced.

While the relationship between anti-Semitism and education is quite strong, an analysis of the trend in acceptance of anti-Semitic beliefs within educational levels (for example, among college graduates) reveals that since 1964 the link between education and anti-Semitism has declined. For example, in 1964 individuals with less than a high school diploma were on average more than three times as likely as college graduates to hold individual anti-Semitic beliefs. By 1981, this ratio had dropped to less than two to one. The decline in the relationship has come about primarily for two reasons. Americans with lower levels of education have become relatively less anti-Semitic; and well-educated Americans have developed increasingly negative attitudes toward Jews in three areas—concern about Jewish power in general and business power in particular and increased criticism of Jewish loyalty to Israel.

Taking attitudes toward Jewish loyalty to Israel as an example, we find that in 1964, 57 percent of non-Jews who had not graduated from high school agreed that "Jews are more loyal to Israel than to America." In 1981, that figure had remained essentially unchanged among those who had not graduated from high school (61 percent agreed). However, among college graduates a quite different picture emerges. In 1964, 12 percent of college graduates believed that Jews are more loyal to Israel than to America. By 1981, that figure had risen to 33 percent. What we see, then, is that while the historic positive association between education and lower levels of anti-Semitism still exists, it has been weakened because of the increased concern among better-educated Americans with Jewish power and Jewish loyalty to Israel.

Table 4.3. Trends in Attitudes toward Jews within Education Levels

	1964				1981			
	Grade school (%)	High school (%)	Some college (%)	College graduate (%)	Grade school (%)	High school (%)	Some college (%)	College graduate (%)
Jews have too much power in the United States.	22	9	4	5	29	20	25	17
Jews don't care what happens to anyone but their own kind.	44	23	16	7	27	27	13	14
Jews are just as honest as other businessmen.	38	31	26	14	29	23	19	12
Jews have too much power in the business world.	43	29	23	17	43	36	39	28
Jews are more loyal to Israel than to United States.	57	32	22	12	61	52	34	33
International banking is pretty much controlled by Jews.	69	44	46	40	50	50	33	31
The trouble with Jewish businessmen is that they are so shrewd and tricky that other people don't have a fair chance in competition.	56	32	25	14	39	27	20	14
Jews stick together too much.	67	55	46	39	60	59	42	44
Jews always like to be at the head of things.	73	57	58	47	57	58	46	41
Jews have a lot of irritating faults.	56	44	43	32	38	32	20	20
Jews are more willing than others to use shady practices to get what they want.	60	43	43	22	48	35	20	17

Note: Based on those with an opinion.

ANTI-SEMITISM AND AGE

While somewhat less dramatic than the effects of education, age is also significantly related to anti-Semitic beliefs. Individuals who are 55 years of age or over are as likely to be prejudiced as they are to be unprejudiced (30 percent prejudiced and 31 percent unprejudiced). On the other hand, those who are 18 to 29 years of age are predominantly unprejudiced (47 percent unprejudiced versus 16 percent prejudiced).

A partial correlation analysis indicates that the apparent effects of age are, in part, actually the effects of education. That is, part of the reason why young people are less prejudiced than older people is that they are better educated, and education, as we have seen, is associated with lower levels of prejudice. The zero-order correlation between age and anti-Semitism is $r = .173$. After controlling for education, the partial correlation between age and anti-Semitism drops to .12. Clearly, while education is a significant factor in relationships between age and anti-Semitism, it is not the only factor or even the principal one. The other critical dimension is the fact that young people are simply generally more tolerant of diversity regardless of their educational background—an issue we will return to in Chapter 6.

One final point worthy of comment is that while the current crop of 18 to 29 year olds are significantly more likely to believe Jews are more loyal to Israel than to America than were 18 to 29 year olds in 1964, on balance, young people today are somewhat less anti-Semitic than were young people in 1964. The implication here is clear. We have evidence for the argument made in Chapter 3 that, as today's young people grow older and displace today's older adults, the process of generational change can be expected to continue.

ANTI-SEMITISM AND RACE

There has been considerable research and discussion on the tension that exists between blacks and Jews.[5] The current study, like others in the past, indicates that blacks are more anti-Semitic than are whites. Overall, 27 percent of blacks can be characterized as prejudiced compared to 22 percent who are unprejudiced, with many (41 percent), particularly those in the South and in rural areas, being neutral. Thus blacks are more likely to be found among the prejudiced

Table 4.4. Trends in Attitudes toward Jews within Age Levels

	Age							
	1964				1981			
	18–29 (%)	30–39 (%)	40–54 (%)	55 and over (%)	18–29 (%)	30–39 (%)	40–54 (%)	55 and over (%)
Jews have too much power in the United States.	7	9	11	20	16	24	23	31
Jews don't care what happens to anyone but their own kind.	23	23	28	42	18	23	16	31
Jews are just as honest as other businessmen.	25	29	30	35	22	24	17	24
Jews have too much power in the business world.	23	25	30	46	29	35	40	46
Jews are more loyal to Israel than to United States.	30	30	33	53	51	44	39	58
International banking is pretty much controlled by Jews.	34	40	56	77	33	40	36	65
The trouble with Jewish businessmen is that they are so shrewd and tricky that other people don't have a fair chance in competition.	32	33	37	53	23	26	20	39
Jews stick together too much.	51	55	56	66	42	52	54	64
Jews always like to be at the head of things.	62	57	58	73	47	53	47	63
Jews have a lot of irritating faults.	41	41	45	58	22	32	26	37
Jews are more willing than others to use shady practices to get what they want.	41	42	46	59	26	32	26	48

Note: Based on those with an opinion.

Table 4.5. Trends in Attitudes toward Jews: Whites versus Blacks among Non-Jews

	Total non-Jews			Whites			Blacks		
	1964 (%)	1981 (%)	Net difference: 1981-1964 (%)	1964 (%)	1981 (%)	Net difference: 1981-1964 (%)	1964 (%)	1981 (%)	Net difference: 1981-1964 (%)
Probably true[a]									
Too much power in United States	13	23	+10	13	20	+7	11	42	+31
Care only about own kind	30	21	-9	27	18	-9	49	43	-6
Not as honest as other businnessmen	29	22	-7	29	17	-10	28	47	+19
Too much power in business world	33	37	+4	35	35	0	22	51	+29
More loyal to Israel than to United States	39	48	+9	38	45	+7	51	63	+12
Control international banking	56	43	-13	52	40	-12	74	67	-7
Shrewd and tricky in business	40	27	-13	38	24	-12	54	45	-9
Have a lot of irritating faults	48	28	-20	46	28	-18	56	36	-20
Use shady practices to get ahead	47	33	-14	45	30	-15	67	58	-9
Stick together too much	58	53	-5	59	52	-7	52	63	+11
Always like to head things	63	52	-11	62	51	-11	70	64	-6
Mean level of anti-Semitism	42.4	35.2	-7.2	40.4	32.7	-7.7	48.5	52.6	+4.1

[a]Items used in anti-Semitism index.
Note: Based on those with an opinion.

than the unprejudiced. Whites, on the other hand, tend to fall among the unprejudiced (47 percent) rather than the prejudiced (20 percent). Blacks are particularly more likely than whites to believe that Jews are unethical in business and have too much power and influence—areas of life that are clearly of critical importance to Black Americans given their economic disenfranchisement.

One critical aspect of black anti-Semitism is that, while prejudice against Jews has declined significantly among whites since 1964, among blacks it has risen slightly because declines in some anti-Semitic beliefs have been offset by large increases in the proportion of blacks who believe Jews have too much power in general, have too much power in the business world, and are dishonest.

Another factor helps explain the absence of a decline in the general level of anti-Semitism among blacks. While generational change and increased education have led to lower levels of anti-Semitism among whites, among blacks, age and anti-Semitism are not highly related ($r = .07$), and the effects of education are significantly less powerful among blacks than among whites ($r = .14$ among blacks versus .25 among whites). As a result of the weak correlations among blacks between age and anti-Semitism and education and anti-Semitism, increased education and generational change have not led to lower levels of anti-Semitism.

BLACK PREJUDICE AGAINST JEWS OR AGAINST WHITES?

One significant finding of the study is that prejudice toward Jews among blacks is often not significantly greater than prejudice against other white groups. In fact, even in the critical area of power, black perception of the level of power of Jews is not significantly greater than the perceived power of Italian Americans. Also, blacks are as likely or more likely to accept Jews as they are Italian Americans as neighbors, political candidates, or marriage partners for their children. The one issue that appears to separate Jews from other ethnic groups in the view of blacks is the perceived business power of Jews: 40 percent believe Jews have too much power in the business world, compared to 28 percent who feel that way about Italian Americans and 17 percent who feel that way about Japanese Americans. The issue of the perceived business power of Jews also ties in with the fact that blacks are more likely than whites to say they resent the economic success of immigrants. The majority (52 percent) of blacks agree that "it bothers me to see immigrants succeeding more than Americans who were born here" compared to only 28 percent of whites.

Overall then, it is clear that prejudice against Jews is in good measure a particular expression of black hostility toward whites in general, or, as James Baldwin has argued, "Negroes are anti-Semitic because they're anti-white."[6] To the extent that black prejudice is uniquely directed against Jews, it appears to stem from economic sources. After fifteen years, the conclusion of Gary Marx's study of the black community stands firm: "the fact of widespread economic contact between Negroes and Jews is certain, and that some hostility may arise from these contacts seems entirely plausible. Thus, while we do not assume that these contacts are the sole source of Negro hostility, it would seem from the data that they are an important source."[7]

SUMMARY

The results of the study indicate that anti-Semitism is most strongly associated with three demographic characteristics: age, education, and race. The level of anti-Semitism is higher among adults who are older, less educated, or black. Education is the strongest demographic correlate of anti-Semitism. Among non-Jews with less than a high school diploma, 33 percent are unprejudiced compared to 61 percent of all college graduates. The effects of age are associated with education, however: even after controlling for education, we found that young adults are significantly less anti-Semitic than those who are older.

Along with education and age, race is the other demographic factor most closely associated with anti-Semitism. One out of five whites can be characterized as prejudiced compared to nearly two out of five (37 percent) blacks. Unlike white anti-Semitism, which has declined somewhat since 1964, the level among blacks has remained essentially the same since 1964.

The nature of anti-Semitic beliefs of blacks extends to virtually all the items in the index. However, it is particularly characteristic of that subset of beliefs that is related to the purported economic power and unethical business practices of Jews. The current analysis strongly suggests that to the extent that black prejudice is uniquely directed against Jews, it appears to stem from economic sources.

NOTES

1. See appendixes B and C for fuller discussion of details of the index.

2. See appendixes B and C for factor analysis and correlation matrix of items measuring anti-Semitic beliefs.

3. See Chapter 5.

4. G. Selznick and S. Steinberg, *The Tenacity of Prejudice* (New York: Harper & Row, 1969), p. 72.

5. See G. Marx, *Protest and Prejudice: A Study of Belief in the Black Community* (New York: Harper & Row, 1967); Selznick and Steinberg, *The Tenacity of Prejudice*, Chapter 7; and J. Baldwin, "Negroes Are Anti-Semitic because They're Anti-White," in *Anti-Semitism in the United States*, L. Dinnerstein, ed. (New York: Holt, Rinehart & Winston, 1971), pp. 125–131.

6. Baldwin, "Negroes Are Anti-Semitic because They're Anti-White," pp. 125–131.

7. Marx, *Protest and Prejudice*, pp. 165–166.

5

ANTI-SEMITISM AND
SOCIAL CONTACT WITH JEWS

It has been 70 years since Robert Park and his colleagues at the University of Chicago began to evolve their theories of racial and ethnic relations. The centerpiece of those theories was a response to the question of what happens "when people of divergent cultures come into contact and conflict."[1] Park's response was a description of a process that begins with social contact and progresses through accommodation, assimilation, and finally amalgamation—an outcome that occurs through intermarriage. With the rise of research on ethnicity in the 1970s, Park's melting pot thesis has been the subject of some debate.[2] However, it continues to be the major theoretical underpinning of much of American thought about race and ethnic relations. While the current study does not address the issues of trends in assimilation or amalgamation, the evidence on social contact and accommodation is quite clear. Social contact between Jews and non-Jews is associated, by and large, with higher levels of social acceptance.

SOCIAL CONTACT BETWEEN JEWS AND NON-JEWS

Given the size of the American Jewish community relative to the black community, contact between Jews and the larger society is greater than is contact between Black Americans or Italian Americans and the larger society. Although blacks outnumber Jews by three or four to one, both groups are almost equally likely to have

46

Table 5.1. Contact with Various Groups in the Total Sample
Exclusive of the Members of the Group Being Described

| | Group being asked about | | | |
	Jews (%)	Italian Americans (%)	Black Americans (%)	Japanese Americans (%)
At the present time, do you come into contact with group in any of the following ways?				
At stores you shop in	58	60	77	44
At work or in business	43	48	61	27
Ever had a close friend who is a member of group	36	47	49	18
Some of the people you know best are members of group	27	39	30	10
At clubs or organizations you belong to	25	30	25	13
In your neighborhood	24	35	33	15
Doctor or dentist is a member of group	15	10	4	4
Someone in family is married to a member of group	10	19	3	2

social contact with members of the larger society in informal, personal settings. For example, 25 percent of non-Jews say they come into contact with Jews in the clubs or organizations to which they belong. Similarly, 25 percent of nonblacks have contact with blacks in the clubs or organizations to which they belong.

Perhaps more important than the general level of social contact between Jews and non-Jews is the character of that contact. The most common form of social contact for each of the groups asked about is impersonal in nature—contact in stores or at work or business. The majority (58 percent) of non-Jews say they come into contact with Jews at the stores in which they shop and four out of ten (43 percent) say they have contact with Jews at work or business. While much of the contact is therefore of a relatively impersonal nature, it is clear that there is also a good deal of highly personal interaction. One in three (36 percent) non-Jews say they have had close friends who are Jews and one in four say they have contact with Jews in clubs or organizations they belong to or in their neighborhood. Since 1964, the quantity of social contact between Jews and non-Jews has not changed dramatically in the areas covered by the questionnaire. Social contact has risen somewhat in clubs or organizations and in neighborhoods and declined in other areas including in shops, with doctors, dentists, and in close friendship.

THE EFFECT OF
BACKGROUND CHARACTERISTICS

Among non-Jews, the most important correlate of social contact with Jews is education. The majority (56 percent) of non-Jews who are college graduates have a high level of contact with Jews. This contrasts sharply with the low level of social contact with Jews among individuals with a low level of education. Overall, only 14 percent of non-Jews with less than a high school education can be characterized as having a high level of social contact with Jews.

More important than the amount of contact with Jews among the well-educated is the nature of their social contact. Non-Jews who are well educated are likely to have more personal contact with Jews. For example, 65 percent of non-Jews who are college graduates say that they have had a close friend who is Jewish compared to 20 percent of non-Jews who did not graduate from high school. College education appears to be a critical breakpoint. Individuals with college education are decisively different in their social relations with Jews from those without a college education. Since World War II, the college experience itself has been, no doubt, an important factor in forging friendships and social contacts across ethnic, racial, and religious lines.

Apart from education, the most important factors associated with social contact with Jews are region, religion, age, and race. Contact with Jews is highest in the Northeast, which, of course, has the highest concentration of Jews. Catholics, who like Jews are more heavily represented in the Northeast, are more likely to have contact with Jews than are Protestants. Also, non-Jews who are 55 years of age and over are significantly less likely to have contact with Jews.

Table 5.2. Social Contact with Jews in Key Groups among
Non-Jews

		Number of types of social contact		
		None (%)	Moderate (%)	High (%)
Total non-Jews	(100%)	26	45	29
Sex				
Men	(100%)	23	45	32
Women	(100%)	28	44	28
Race				
White	(100%)	25	44	31
Black	(100%)	26	53	21
Religion				
Catholic	(100%)	20	44	36
Protestant	(100%)	29	47	24
Age				
18–29 years	(100%)	23	45	32
30–39 years	(100%)	26	43	31
40–54 years	(100%)	16	46	38
55 years and over	(100%)	36	42	22
Education				
Did not graduate from high school	(100%)	39	47	14
High school graduate	(100%)	26	50	24
Some college	(100%)	15	41	44
College graduate	(100%)	12	32	56
Region				
Northeast	(100%)	10	43	47
Midwest	(100%)	28	43	29
South	(100%)	37	44	19
West	(100%)	21	48	31

SOCIAL CONTACT AND ANTI-SEMITISM

Social contact with Jews is clearly associated with lower levels of
anti-Semitic prejudice. For example, one out of two (49 percent) of
the unprejudiced say they have a close friend who is Jewish compared to 32 percent of individuals who are prejudiced. Similarly, 33
percent of the unprejudiced have contact with Jews in their clubs or
organizations compared to 20 percent of the prejudiced.

Table 5.3. Anti-Semitism and Contact with Jews among Non-Jews

	Total non-Jews (%)	Prejudiced (%)	Neutrals (%)	Unprejudiced (%)
Where non-Jews come into contact with Jews				
At stores you shop in	58	56	46	68
At work or in business	43	48	32	49
Ever had a close friend who is Jewish	36	32	21	49
Some of the people you know best are Jewish	27	21	17	37
In clubs or organizations you belong to	25	20	17	33
In your neighborhood	24	24	13	32
Doctor or dentist is Jewish	15	18	8	17
Someone in family is married to a Jew	10	8	5	13
Number of types of contact with Jews				
No contact	26	26	38	16
1–2 types	32	34	32	30
3–4 types	24	22 ⎫ 40	21 ⎫ 30	28 ⎫ 54
5–8 types	18	18 ⎭	9 ⎭	26 ⎭

The process of accommodation that is associated with social contact appears to depend not upon the amount of social contact but upon its character. Interaction between Jews and non-Jews in business or in such impersonal roles as a doctor-patient relationship does not appear to be associated with lower levels of prejudice. Indeed the level of contact between Jews and non-Jews in business settings appears to be nearly identical for prejudiced and unprejudiced individuals. Given the cross sectional nature of the current survey, we can say little about the causal nature of the relationship between social contact and reduced prejudice. However our general assessment is that the conclusion of Glock and his colleagues with respect to adolescent prejudice probably holds for adults as well.

In settings where Jews are present and where opportunities for inter-religious friendships are taken up, the net effect is a reduction in the incidence of anti-Semitism. At the same time, however the gross amount of anti-Semitism is greater where there is a Jewish presence than in a community where there is not. Moreover, the larger the Jewish presence the greater the anti-Semitism.[3]

This last point receives further support in our own earlier reported finding that anti-Semitism is higher in larger cities (where there is more likely to be a significant Jewish presence) than in small towns or rural areas.

SOCIAL CONTACT AND ANTI-SEMITISM AMONG BLACKS

The level of social contact between Jews and blacks is somewhat lower than that between Jews and non-Jews in general—22 percent of blacks have a high degree of social contact with Jews compared to 31 percent of whites. Again, more important than this generally lower level of contact is the nature of black-Jewish interaction. As Gary Marx (1967) and others have argued, there is evidence to indicate that, because of their own historically marginal status, Jews have developed a "middleman" role between the black community and the larger white society in such roles as merchants, teachers, principals, and social workers.[4] This position receives some support from the fact that contact with Jews is quite similar among blacks and whites when it comes to such settings as work, stores, or doctor-patient relations. However, in more personal settings such as friendships or clubs or organizations, blacks are significantly less likely to have contact with Jews.

Given the nature of black-Jewish interaction, therefore, it should come as no great surprise that black social contact with Jews is not associated with lower levels of anti-Semitism. While among whites social contact with Jews is associated with lower levels of anti-Semitism, among blacks, on the contrary, increased social contact with Jews is associated with higher levels of anti-Semitism. Overall the correlation of white-Jewish social contact and anti-Semitism is ($r = -.13$); as interaction increases, anti-Semitism declines. However, the correlation of black-Jewish interaction and anti-Semitism is ($r = +.16$), indicating that as black-Jewish interaction increases, so too does anti-Semitism.

The current study generally supports the idea that social contact is linked to social acceptance. Individuals with more social contact with Jews are less likely to be prejudiced in their views about Jews. The link between social contact and reduced prejudice is particularly strong when it comes to more personal types of contact including friendships and contacts in clubs and organizations. Because black-Jewish contact is often of an impersonal nature, it does not appear to be associated with reduced prejudice. Indeed, black-Jewish social contact appears to be associated with increased prejudice among blacks.

SUMMARY

Given the size of the American Jewish community relative to the number of Black Americans or Italian Americans, contact between Jews and the larger society is greater than that between the larger society and Black Americans or Italian Americans. Since the mid-1960s, the level of Jewish/non-Jewish interaction has not changed dramatically—it has risen slightly in some areas and declined in others.

The link between social contact and social acceptance is supported by the current study. Individuals with positive attitudes toward Jews are significantly more likely to have contact with them in a variety of ways including at clubs and organizations and in close friendships.

This link between higher levels of social contact and lower levels of anti-Semitism is not universal, however. Among blacks, a higher level of association with Jews is correlated with greater anti-Semitism. The data suggest, however, that it is not black Jewish contact per se that stimulates this but the nature of the black Jewish contact. Contact between blacks and Jews is more likely to be impersonal (for example, with doctor, dentist, or shopkeeper) rather than truly social contact (for example, clubs, organizations, or marriage).

NOTES

1. R. Park, *Race and Culture* (Glencoe, Ill.: Free Press, 1955), p. 5.
2. See M. Novak, *The Rise of the Unmeltable Ethnics* (New York: Macmillan, 1971); N. Glazer and D. P. Moynihan, *Beyond the Melting Pot* (Cambridge: MIT Press, 1964).
3. C. Glock et al., *Adolescent Prejudice* (New York: Harper & Row, 1975), p. 130.
4. G. Marx, *Protest and Prejudice: A Study of Belief in the Black Community* (New York: Harper & Row, 1967), p. 154.

6

THE TOLERANCE OF DIVERSITY

One of the most dramatic changes that has taken place in U.S. society since 1964 is the increased tolerance of different attitudes, values, and life-styles. The increased acceptance of diversity has affected all of the nation's social institutions including the family, the school, and the media. The law has also changed quite significantly to reflect these changing norms. Since the mid-1960s the courts have provided legal support for the rights of women to "palimony" after ending an unmarried sexual relationship, the "right to die" for the terminally ill, and the right of a woman to have an abortion. Underlying many of these new rights has been a changing climate of public opinion that has grown increasingly tolerant of diversity.[1]

This growth in tolerance finds its expression in the current study in increased acceptance of diversity of several types. Compared to the 1964 baseline, the results of our survey indicate that Americans now express more acceptance of atheists, individuals with beards, and the right of foreigners to "maintain their foreign ways." Also, Americans are less likely to endorse the superiority of the "American way of life." This increased tolerance for diversity has sometimes been quite dramatic. In 1964, 60 percent of all adults believed that a man who admitted in public that he did not believe in God should not be allowed to teach in a public school.

By 1981 that number had dropped to 24 percent, a decline of 36 percent over a period of 17 years. Similarly, in 1964, two out of three (67 percent) Americans believed that "foreigners who come to

America should give up their foreign ways and learn to be like other Americans." By 1981 that figure, while still high, had dropped to 50 percent.

This growth in acceptance of different viewpoints and life-styles has not been universal and does not necessarily imply an inevitable decline in conflict. Indeed, since 1964 there has been a growth in the proportion of Americans who say they are bothered by the economic success of immigrants, which indicates that the basis of economic conflict may be growing. Nevertheless, on balance, the trend has been striking and is consistent with findings of many studies conducted by Yankelovich, Skelly and White, Inc. that have found growing social pluralism in the United States since the late 1960s.

XENOPHOBIA

An examination of a number of the items measuring tolerance for diversity in the current survey indicates the presence of a xenophobia factor composed of the following four items:[2]

It bothers me to see immigrants succeeding more than Americans who were born here. (agree)
Nothing in other countries can beat the American way of life. (agree)
Foreigners who come to live in America should give up their foreign ways and learn to be like other Americans. (agree)
The illegal alien situation is one of the most serious problems in America. (agree)

An analysis of a trichotomized version of the xenophobia index indicates that xenophobia is highest among those who are:

older (55 years and over);
less educated;
living in small towns;
politically conservative;
Protestant (especially Baptist);
living in the south.

On the other hand, xenophobia is lowest among those who are:

Table 6.1. Demographic Profile of the Xenophobia Index

		High (%)	Medium (%)	Low (%)
Total	(100%)	35	36	29
Sex				
Men	(100%)	34	36	30
Women	(100%)	35	36	29
Race				
White	(100%)	35	36	29
Black	(100%)	37	35	28
Religion				
Total Non-Jews	(100%)	27	34	39
Catholic	(100%)	31	41	28
Protestant	(100%)	40	35	25
Baptist	(100%)	51	32	17
Jews	(100%)	27	34	39
Age				
18–29 years	(100%)	23	35	42
30–39 years	(100%)	30	35	35
40–54 years	(100%)	32	40	28
55 years and over	(100%)	52	36	12
Education				
Less than high school graduate	(100%)	50	39	11
High school graduate	(100%)	39	35	26
Some college	(100%)	19	40	41
College graduate	(100%)	15	30	55
Region				
Northeast	(100%)	35	39	36
Midwest	(100%)	31	36	33
South	(100%)	47	31	22
West	(100%)	30	42	28
Political outlook				
Conservative	(100%)	45	34	21
Moderate	(100%)	30	37	33
Liberal/radical	(100%)	22	38	40
Type of place				
Central city	(100%)	31	32	37
Suburb	(100%)	32	41	27
Rural/small town	(100%)	44	33	23

young (18 to 29 years);
better educated;
liberal;
Jews.

XENOPHOBIA AND ANTI-SEMITISM

There is a long tradition in social science research that links prejudice in general and anti-Semitism in particular to a general tendency toward ethnocentrism and intolerance of diversity. The Ethnocentrism (e) Scale developed in 1950 for *The Authoritarian Personality* proved to be highly correlated with anti-Semitism. More recently, the Index of Cultural Diversity[3] developed by Selznick and Steinberg was also found to be highly related to anti-Semitism.

In the current analysis, we again find that rejection of the foreign is highly related to acceptance of anti-Semitic beliefs. The overall correlation between xenophobia and the anti-Semitism index is fairly strong (r = .365). Among individuals who are high in xenophobia, 38 percent are prejudiced and 33 percent are unprejudiced. In contrast, among those low in xenophobia, only 12 percent are prejudiced compared to 58 percent who are unprejudiced. Acceptance of anti-Semitic beliefs is, to a considerable extent, rejection of the foreign in general. It is clear then, that one important reason for the decline

Table 6.2. The Impact of Xenophobia among Non-Jews

	Total non-Jews (%)	Xenophobia								
		Total			High school graduates or less			Some college/ college graduates		
		High (%)	Medium (%)	Low (%)	High (%)	Medium (%)	Low (%)	High (%)	Medium (%)	Low (%)
Anti-Semitism index										
Prejudiced	23	38	18	12	39	18	15	29	16	10
Neutrals	32	29	36	28	31	43	40	26	22	19
Unprejudiced	45	33	46	60	30	39	45	45	62	71

in anti-Semitic prejudice in the past 20 years is the growing acceptance of social pluralism in general.

While demographic factors such as education and age play an important role in explaining xenophobia and its link to anti-Semitism, the relationship is not reducible to these demographic factors. For example, when we control for the effects of education by examining the xenophobia–anti-Semitism relationship only among non-Jews with some college education or more, we find that there is still a strong relationship. Only 10 percent of the college educated who are low in xenophobia are prejudiced compared to 29 percent among those high in xenophobia.

While the relationship between xenophobia and anti-Semitism is reduced somewhat by controlling for the fact that younger and better-educated non-Jews are less xenophobic and less prejudiced, these controls do not reduce the relationship dramatically. In fact, after controlling for education, we find that the correlation of anti-Semitism and xenophobia drops from .365 to .303. After we control for education, age, race, income, city size, place of origin, and a number of other background factors, the partial correlation of anti-Semitism and xenophobia only drops to .287. The relationship between xenophobia and anti-Semitism remains quite strong then, even after we control for this large array of background factors. The conclusion we draw from these data is that xenophobia is more than a proxy for the effects of background factors. It has important independent significance in explaining anti-Semitism. Consequently, anti-Semitism must be understood as partially the reflection of a more general fear of the foreign and unfamiliar.

ANTI-SEMITISM, XENOPHOBIA AND ATTITUDES TOWARD BLACK AMERICANS

Further support for the relationships between anti-Semitism and a more general xenophobia comes from the fact that individuals who are anti-Semitic are also more likely to hold negative views about Black Americans, Italian Americans and Japanese Americans. For example, white non-Jews who are anti-Semitic are more likely to view blacks as unambitious, pushy, and having too much power. They are also more likely to put social distance between themselves and Black Americans when it comes to politics, marriage, and living

Table 6.3. Anti-Semitism and Attitudes toward Blacks among White Non-Jews

	Total white non-Jews (%)	Prej-udiced (%)	Neutrals (%)	Unprej-udiced (%)
Attitudes toward blacks				
Blacks are less ambitious.	43	56	43	36
Blacks try and push in where they are not wanted.	45	62	41	41
Blacks are very family oriented.	46	45	41	50
Blacks have too much power in the United States.	7	26	16	12
Blacks have too much influence in politics.	10	19	7	9
Blacks have too much influence in government in general.	11	21	6	10
Social distance/acceptance of blacks				
Would object strongly/somewhat to own child marrying a black	70	85	71	63
Would prefer not to have any blacks in the neighborhood	31	48	25	30
Would be bothered very much/ somewhat by my political party nominating a black for president	35	55	27	35

together in the same neighborhood. This close tie between anti-Semitism and antiblack sentiments indicates that with anti-Semitism we are dealing to a large extent with prejudice against minorities in general.

It is sadly ironic that two of the most anti-Semitic groups uncovered in the current study are Black Americans and whites who are highly xenophobic. The irony, of course, is that the tension in black-Jewish relations serves to impede the necessary attempts to build coalitions of common interest to fight intolerance of all kinds.

SUMMARY

One of the most dramatic changes that has taken place in U.S. society in the past 20 years is the growth in acceptance of diversity of life-styles and beliefs.

The current study indicates that Americans now express more acceptance of atheists, individuals with beards, and the rights of foreigners to "maintain their foreign ways." Americans are also less likely today to chauvinistically support the superiority of the American way of life. This increasing acceptance of the "foreign" is at the heart of the increased tolerance of Jews in America. Xenophobia is, in fact, the single most powerful correlate of anti-Semitism—four out of ten (38 percent) non-Jews who are highly xenophobic are also anti-Semitic, compared to only one in ten (12 percent) who are prejudiced among those low in xenophobia.

The association between xenophobia and anti-Semitism is also supported by the fact that anti-Semitic attitudes are correlated with antiblack attitudes. For example, two out of three (62 percent) anti-Semitic individuals believe that blacks are trying to push in where they are not wanted compared to four out of ten (41 percent) non-anti-Semitic individuals.

NOTES

1. The following articles document changes in attitudes over the past ten to twenty years that demonstrate the increased tolerance for different attitudes, values, and life-styles: "The Polls: Abortion," *Public Opinion Quarterly*, Winter 1977–78, pp. 553–564; "The Polls: Homosexuality," *Public Opinion Quarterly*, Summer 1978, pp. 265–276; "The Polls: Changing Attitudes Toward Euthanasia," *Public Opinion Quarterly*, Spring 1980, pp. 123–128; "The Polls: Women At Work," *Public Opinion Quarterly*, Summer 1977, pp. 268–277; "Racial Attitudes: Tensions Relax," *Public Opinion*, October/November 1980, p. 28.

2. See Appendix C for details of the factor analysis of items measuring xenophobia and description of index construction.

3. T. W. Adorno et al., *The Authoritarian Personality* (New York: W. W. Norton, 1950); C. Selznick and S. Steinberg, *The Tenacity of Prejudice* (New York: Harper & Row, 1969).

One of the items in the Selznick and Steinberg Index of Tolerance for Cultural Diversity was reproduced as part of the measure of xenophobia. It is the item: "foreigners who come to live in America should give up their foreign ways and learn to be like other Americans."

7

ANTI-SEMITISM AND THE
CURRENT ECONOMIC AND
POLITICAL ENVIRONMENT

Many individuals and organizations who are interested in the position of Jews in the United States have expressed concern about the possible impact on American Jews of current domestic and international economic and political problems. Writing in the *Jewish Times*, David Friedman put it this way: "many American Jews are uneasy. They do not know whether to blame [their uneasiness] on the economic situation, whether Arab oil bears some responsibility or whether their support of Israel and the worldwide attack which Israel is under has some bearing."[1]

This concern about the possibility that Jews will be scapegoats for economic and political turmoil is grounded in many historical precedents that are well known, including the pograms of Tsarist Russia and of Germany of the 1930s. More recently, there is evidence that the Polish government used anti-Semitism as a weapon in its battle against Solidarity and political dissidents. Indeed, after the declaration of martial law in Poland in the winter of 1981, the state-censored press was reported to be using "anti-Semitism which has a long history in Poland to attack KOR [dissident organization] and through it, Solidarity."[2]

While the political and economic turmoil in the United States has not been as dramatic as the situation in Poland and elsewhere, there has been a significant amount of economic dislocation and political change. Many of these political and economic factors could be hypothesized to have an effect on anti-Semitism. In the economic sphere, Jews might have become one of the scapegoats for the weak national economy with its alternating periods of unemployment and high inflation. In the political sphere, the growing political conservatism and the Arab-Israeli conflict are other important features of the last decade that might also be hypothesized to have an impact on anti-Semitism in the United States.

This chapter examines these and other economic and political phenomena and concludes that, at the present time, they have had little impact.

ANTI-SEMITISM AND DOMESTIC AND INTERNATIONAL CONCERNS

One means of testing the impact of economic and political concerns on the level of anti-Semitism in the United States is to determine whether or not those, for example, who are worried a great deal about unemployment, a recession, or an energy shortage are more likely to be anti-Semitic. The results of the current study indicate that in early 1981 there was widespread concern in the United States about recession, an energy shortage, and the possibility of war in the Middle East. Indeed one out of two Americans indicated they were "worried a lot" about each of these potential problems. However, despite these widespread economic and political concerns, there

Table 7.1. Anti-Semitism and Current Domestic and International Concerns among Non-Jews

	Total non-Jews (%)	Prejudiced (%)	Neutrals (%)	Unprejudiced (%)
Worried a lot about				
Losing your job because of the economy	27	26	30	25
A recession in the country	50	53	53	46
An energy shortage	51	51	55	48
Another war in the Middle East	47	47	50	45
The possibility of a world war	47	50	49	44

appears to be little evidence of anti-Jewish scapegoatism. Concern about the problems of the economy and the related issues of oil and the Middle East are not significantly tied to anti-Semitism. Individuals who are prejudiced are not significantly more likely than the unprejudiced to be worried a lot about these problems. For example, 51 percent of the prejudiced are worried a lot about an energy shortage compared to 48 percent of the unprejudiced. Similarly, one out of four of both the prejudiced and the unprejudiced are worried a lot about losing their job because of the economy. The interpretation here is clear: there is little or no evidence of a backlash of anti-Jewish sentiment as a result of the nation's economic problems in general or the problems of energy and the Middle East in particular.

ANTI-SEMITISM AND SOCIAL MOBILITY

Another perspective on the possible impact of economic factors on anti-Semitism is provided by examining the relationship between social mobility and anti-Semitism. It has been argued that the downwardly mobile need a scapegoat for their personal failure and consequently are more likely to be anti-Semitic.[3]

Table 7.2. Social Mobility and Anti-Semitism among Non-Jews

	Total non-Jews (%)	Downwardly mobile (%)	Stationary (%)	Upwardly mobile (%)
Anti-Semitism index				
Prejudiced	23	28	23	22
Neutrals	32	26	31	33
Unprejudiced	45	46	46	45

Like the 1964 baseline, the current study finds little support for this thesis. One in ten (9 percent) individuals describe their socioeconomic status as being lower than that of their family when they were growing up. In terms of their attitudes toward Jews, these individuals who are downwardly mobile are remarkably similar to those who have been upwardly mobile or stationary.[4]

ANTI-SEMITISM AND POLITICAL
ATTITUDES AND BEHAVIOR

Perhaps the best known attempt to understand anti-Semitism in the United States is the classic study, *The Authoritarian Personality*, sponsored by the American Jewish Committee and conducted at the University of California at Berkeley by T. W. Adorno and colleagues.[5] The central theme of the book was the delineation of an authoritarian character type. Individuals who were authoritarian personalities were likely to be anti-Semitic, antidemocratic, and politically and economically conservative.

Table 7.3. Political Outlook and Anti-Semitism among Non-Jews

	Total non-Jews (%)	Total			High school graduate or less			Some college/ college graduates		
		Conservative (%)	Moderate (%)	Liberal (%)	Conservative (%)	Moderate (%)	Liberal (%)	Conservative (%)	Moderate (%)	Liberal (%)
Anti-Semitism index										
Prejudiced	23	27	18	22	30	20	27	18	13	14
Neutral	32	31	34	27	36	41	34	22	23	18
Unprejudiced	45	42	48	51	34	39	39	60	64	68

Published in 1950, *The Authoritarian Personality* would have supported the hypothesis that anti-Semitism should be associated with such right-wing ideologues as Senator Joseph McCarthy and Governor George Wallace. However, as William Schneider has pointed out, McCarthy, Wallace, and more recent right-wing ideologues such as Jerry Falwell have not been openly associated with anti-Semitic sentiments.

European history and the record of American groups like the Ku Klux Klan and the Coughlinites in the 1930's have taught Jews to associate anti-Semitic backlash with the right. This association led many to fear that conservatives would resent Jewish activism in the various civil rights and New Left movements and would use this resentment as a pretext for a new wave of anti-Semitism. The interesting point is that this right-wing anti-Semitic backlash failed to materialize. Jews were understandably fearful of the [Joseph] McCarthy, Goldwater, and Wallace movements, of the rise to prominency of conservative Republicans like Spiro Agnew and Ronald Reagan, and of the emergence of "cop candidates" and law-and-order protest movements in many American cities. But the fact is that these right-wing figures, Joseph McCarthy and George Wallace included, conscientiously avoided the exploitation of anti-Semitism among their followers. Indeed, some candidates of the New Right have made explicit overtures to Jews, arguing that Jews should consider their self-interest and not merely their ideology. The anti-Semitic and anti-zionist backlash that finally did materialize came from an entirely different direction. It came from the left.[6]

Given the fact that since World War II political leaders in the United States have, almost universally, not attempted to get political mileage out of anti-Semitic positions, it should come as no surprise that anti-Semitism is not strongly tied to political outlook. Twenty-seven percent of self-described conservatives are prejudiced compared to 22 percent of liberals. Further analysis indicates that even this weak relationship is due to the fact that liberals are likely to be somewhat younger and better educated and therefore somewhat less prejudiced against Jews. For example, among those who are high school graduates or less, 30 percent of the conservatives are prejudiced compared to 27 percent of the liberals. In terms of the correlation and partial correlation analysis, we find that the zero order correlation between political outlook and anti-Semitism is .06; anti-Semitism increases slightly as political conservatism increases. The relationship is relatively weak, however, and after we control for education it drops still further to .03.

Consistent with the finding that there is little relationship between political outlook and anti-Semitism is the finding that non-Jews who have grown more conservative in recent years are no more likely to be anti-Semitic than are non-Jews who have grown more liberal. Also, while they remain more liberal than non-Jews, Jews are as likely as non-Jews to say they have grown more conservative in recent years.

Support for the relative unimportance of political attitudes in explaining the level of anti-Semitism is also provided by the absence of any significant relationship between anti-Semitism and the vote in the 1980 presidential election. Forty four percent of Carter supporters can be characterized as unprejudiced and 24 percent are prejudiced. Among Reagan voters, 48 percent are unprejudiced and 23 percent are prejudiced. This is related to the question of the Jewish vote in that election. On the basis of a CBS–New York Times exit poll and a variety of other sources, Milton Himmelfarb concludes that:

> Jews are still on the liberal side of the political terrain—which, has shifted to the right. And they still worry about Israel.
> What was new [in the 1980 election] was very new: fewer than half [of all Jews] voted for the Democrat. The most important cause of this change was the desire for a strong, resolute America and a secure Israel.[7]

Another important political change that has taken place since 1964 is the growing knowledge of and support for the constitutional guarantees provided by the Bill of Rights. In 1964, only one out of two Americans were aware that Congress cannot "pass a law saying that the president must be a man who believes in God." By 1981, awareness of the constitutionally guaranteed separation of church and state had risen to 65 percent. Similarly, in 1964, two out of three (65 percent) Americans were aware that "Congress cannot pass a law saying that groups who disagree with our form of government could not hold public meetings or make speeches." By 1981, that figure had risen to 72 percent. Knowledge of these constitutional guarantees is strongly tied to lower levels of prejudice, indicating

Table 7.4. Knowledge of and Support for the Constitution[8]

	Freedom of speech/ assembly		Separation of church and state	
	1964 (%)	1981 (%)	1964 (%)	1981 (%)
Knowledgeable	65	72	50	65
Not knowledgeable	35	28	50	35
Supportive	80	80	54	62
Not supportive	20	20	46	38
(Not sure)	(4)	(12)	(3)	(8)

Note: Support based on those with an opinion.

that a better educated, more democratic population has grown increasingly aware of the rights of minorities, particularly the rights of atheists.

In conclusion, there appears to be little support in the contemporary United States for *The Authoritarian Personality* thesis that links conservatism and anti-Semitism. As Roger Brown and others have pointed out, the "authors of the 1950 study were not much interested in what has come to be called authoritarianism of the left."[9] It is interesting to note that more recent analysis of anti-Semitism in America regards left-wing authoritarianism as more of a threat to Jews than right-wing authoritarianism.

The following quotation from *The New Anti-Semitism* briefly summarizes the concern of many Jews about the anti-Semitism of the left.

> The Radical Left, comprising elements of the New and Old Left, poses a threat to the Jewish people. It is committed to the liquidation of Israel. And in attempting to fulfill that commitment it has turned its fire on those who support Israel's existence as a Jewish state—principally Jews—while it warmly acclaims and is virtually allied with those seeking Israel's demise—Arabs, their friends in the communist world and others espousing the cause of "Third World" peoples defined by them as including the downtrodden of Asia, Africa, Latin America and the Middle East, and American blacks.[10]

While the concern of some intellectuals about political anti-Semitism during the past 40 years has moved from the right to the left, what is no doubt more important is that for the vast majority of Americans anti-Semitism is not tied to political ideology and is not a significant political force.

SUMMARY

Many individuals and organizations interested in the position of Jews in America have expressed concern about the possible impact of current domestic and international economic and political problems on American Jews. The current study suggests that, at the present time, these economic and political problems have had little impact on the level of anti-Semitism in America.

Individuals with anti-Semitic prejudices are not more likely to be concerned about the economy, energy shortages, or the possibility of a war in the Middle East.

When it comes to political outlook, self-described liberals are somewhat more likely to be firmly non-anti-Semitic. However, the relationship is quite small (conservatives 42 percent unprejudiced, liberals 51 percent), and the greater tolerance of liberals is largely explained by their higher levels of education. Also, the increasing political conservatism of recent years among many Americans is not related to anti-Semitism. In fact, Jews are as likely as non-Jews to have grown more conservative.

NOTES

1. D. Friedman, "The Disease Is Still Malignant," Brookline, Mass., *Jewish Times*, August 27, 1981, p. 20.

2. New York *Times*, "In a Troubled Poland, Jews Again seem to be Made Scapegoats," January 9, 1981, p. 6.

3. B. Bettelheim and M. Janowitz, *Dynamics of Prejudice: A Psychological and Sociological Study of Veterans* (New York: Harper, 1950).

4. Difference between own self described socio-economic status and self description of socio-economic status of own parents while growing up.

5. T. W. Adorno et al., *The Authoritarian Personality* (New York: W. W. Norton, 1950).

6. William Schneider, "Anti-Semitism: A Report on American Public Opinion," December 1978, pp. 108–109 (mimeographed). See also Seymour Martin Lipset and Earl Raab, *The Politics of Unreason: Right Wing Extremism in America 1880-1970* (New York: Harper & Row, 1970).

7. M. Himmelfarb, "Are Jews Becoming More Republican?" *Commentary* 72 (August 1981): 31.

8. See question 4a–5c in questionnaire.

9. Roger Brown, *Social Psychology* (New York: Free Press, 1965), p. 479.

10. Arnold Forster and Benjamin Epstein, *The New Anti-Semitism* (New York: McGraw Hill, 1974), p. 125.

8

RELIGIOUS BELIEFS, RELIGIOUS BEHAVIOR, AND ANTI-SEMITISM

One of the most controversial theses about the causes of anti-Semitism in the past 15 years has been the proposed link of Christianity and Christian belief with anti-Semitism. This chapter explores this controversial area through an analysis of four basic themes:

trends in religious behavior;
the impact of religious behavior on anti-Semitism;
trends in religious beliefs;
the impact of religious belief on anti-Semisitm.

TRENDS IN RELIGIOUS BEHAVIOR

One of the most dramatic trends in U.S. life over the past two decades has been the declining role of religion. While there is some evidence that this decline has halted in recent years, analysis of trend data gathered by the Gallup Organization[1] indicates that over the past 20 years the decline in traditional religious ritual observance and belief has been substantial.

First, the proportion of Americans who say they have "no religious preference" quadrupled between 1967, when it was 2 percent, and 1979, when the comparable figure was 8 percent. The 1980 figure is 7 percent.

Second, church and synagogue attendance dropped from a high of 49 percent attending on a weekly basis in 1958 to a 1980 low of 40 percent. The decline was particularly dramatic among Catholics, 74 percent of whom attended weekly in 1958 compared to 53 percent in 1980.

Table 8.1. Trends in Religious Behavior

	1964 (%)		1981 (%)	
Religious affiliation				
Protestant	68		58	
Catholic	26		28	
Jewish	3		3	
Other	1		1	
None	2		8	
No answer	0		2	
Frequency of attending worship services				
Every week/several times a week	42	50	30	38
Nearly every week	8		8	
2–3 times a month	10		8	
About once a month	8		5	
Several times a year	11		14	
About once or twice a year	11		10	
Less than once a year	4		7	
Never/no answer[a]	6		18	

[a]Includes those with no religious affiliation.

Third, on a more personal level, the percentage of Americans who say that religion is very important in their own lives has dropped significantly among Catholics, Protestants, and Jews. In 1965, 74 percent of Protestants regarded religion as "very important"; by 1980 that figure had dropped to 61 percent. Similarly, in 1965, 76 percent of Catholics regarded religion as very important, and by 1980 that figure had dropped to 56 percent.

The evidence uncovered by the Gallup Organization is also supported by the current study. Since 1964, there has been a decline in the proportion of Americans who describe themselves as Protestants and an increase in those who have no religious affiliation. The Gallup findings on declining church attendance are confirmed in the current effort. In 1964, 50 percent of all Americans attended religious services nearly every week. By 1981, that figure had dropped to 38 percent.

While the significance of the rise of fundamentalism and the advent of electronic churches has been the subject of a great deal of discussion in recent years, it is clear from the preceding data that these groups have been fighting against the prevailing climate of opinion in the United States. As Daniel Yankelovich has argued, "the Moral Majority draws its vitality from a concern shared by millions of Americans. . . . What is this concern? It is that Americans are growing ever more uneasy about the influence of the prevailing moral climate on their children."[2] It is precisely because they are battling against the main currents of American culture that the fundamentalists emerged in the late 1970s and early 1980s as a controversial group.

THE IMPACT OF RELIGIOUS BEHAVIOR ON ANTI-SEMITISM

The frequency of attending worship services among non-Jews does not appear to be a particularly important factor in explaining anti-Semitic attitudes. In fact, apart from the somewhat lower level of prejudice among non-Jews who attend services less than once a year, there is no consistent relationship between church attendance and anti-Semitic prejudice.

When it comes to religious affiliation, there is little difference in the level of anti-Semitism between the two major Christian affiliations. Among Protestants, 45 percent are unprejudiced and 22 percent are prejudiced. Among Catholics, 43 percent are unprejudiced

Table 8.2. Church Attendance and Anti-Semitism

		Anti-Semitism index		
		Prejudiced (%)	Neutral (%)	Unprejudiced (%)
Total non-Jews	(100%)	23	32	45
Frequency of church attendance				
Every week or more often	(100%)	21	34	45
Nearly every week	(100%)	26	39	35
2–3 times a month	(100%)	21	37	42
About once a month	(100%)	31	29	40
Several times a year	(100%)	26	36	38
About once or twice a year	(100%)	29	27	44
Less than once a year/ never	(100%)	15	31	54

Table 8.3. Religious Affiliation and Anti-Semitism

		Anti-Semitism index		
		Prejudiced (%)	Neutral (%)	Unprejudiced (%)
Total	(100%)	22	33	45
Total religious affiliation				
Protestant	(100%)	22	33	45
Baptist	(100%)	26	36	38
Methodist	(100%)	24	33	43
Presbyterian/Episcopal				
Unitarian	(100%)	21	34	45
Other Protestant	(100%)	21	34	45
Catholic	(100%)	25	32	43
None	(100%)	21	15	64

and 25 percent are prejudiced. There is, however, significant variation among the Protestant denominations. Baptists are significantly more likely to be anti-Semitic while the traditional "liberal" Protestant sects (Presbyterians, Episcopalians, and Unitarians) are less likely to be so. These denominational differences are, however, largely the result of the large demographic differences that divide the Protestant sects along social class lines. For example, while 19 percent of the members of the "liberal" Protestant sects have less than a full high school education, among the Baptists, nearly one out of two (48 percent) have less than a high school diploma. It is education, race, and other demographic differences that account for the higher level of anti-Semitism among the Baptists rather than the direct effect of religion.

TRENDS IN RELIGIOUS BELIEFS

Consistently with the decline in religious behavior that has taken place since 1964, there has been a decline in the orthodoxy of religious belief. Americans today are less likely to believe that religion is extremely important and more likely to have doubts about whether God exists. In 1964, 77 percent of all Americans said they "believe

Table 8.4. Trends in Religious Beliefs

	1964 (%)	1981 (%)	Net difference: 1981–1964 (%)
Believe God exists and have no doubt about it	77	62	−15
Believe that a person who does not accept Jesus cannot be saved	51	38	−13
Believe religion is extremely important	50	38	−12
Absolutely/pretty sure that there is life after death	79	76	−3
Absolutely/pretty sure there is a devil	79	76	−3
Describe self as Born Again Christian	—[a]	23	n.a.[b]

[a]Not asked.
[b]Not applicable.

God exists and have no doubts about it." By 1981, that figure had dropped to 62 percent. Also, compared to 1964, non-Jews are less likely to believe "a person who does not accept Jesus cannot be saved" and less likely to believe that Jews are being punished by God for rejecting Jesus" (20 percent in 1964 compared to 13 percent in 1981).

Despite the downward trend in religious belief, it is clear that religion continues to be a vital force in U.S. society:

Three out of four Americans (76 percent) are absolutely sure or pretty sure that there is life beyond death.
Three out of four are absolutely or pretty sure that there is a devil.
Six out of ten (62 percent) believe that God exists and have no doubts about it.
One in four (23 percent) describe themselves as Born Again Christians.

THE IMPACT OF RELIGIOUS BELIEF ON ANTI-SEMITISM

In their summary of recent research on anti-Semitism, Quinley and Glock conclude:

The acceptance of Orthodox Christian beliefs leads to a particularistic religious orientation in which only right-thinking Christians are seen as saved and all others are damned. These views, in turn, are associated with hostile feelings toward Jews—which have both a historical dimension (Jews being held responsible for the Crucifixion) and a contemporary effect (Jews being condemned for their rejection of Jesus as Savior). Such religious beliefs, finally are associated with similar forms of anti-Semitism. Christian laypersons and ministers holding these religious conceptions are disproportionately prejudiced in their attitudes toward Jews.[3]

These conclusions are based primarily on an analysis of the work of Selznick and Steinberg, Glock and Stark, and Stark and colleagues and result in one of the more controversial hypotheses about the causes of anti-Semitism. The controversy concerns the question of whether Christian orthodoxy is a cause of higher levels of anti-Semitism (as Glock and Stark have argued), or whether other factors are linked to both Christian orthodoxy and anti-Semitism, as has been argued by Middleton and by Roof.[4]

In order to examine the relationship between religious belief and anti-Semitism, the current study made use of two separate measures of religious beliefs: a general religious conviction index and a measure of Christian fundamentalist belief.

The measure of religious conviction was based on three items:[5]

the strength of conviction regarding the existence of God;
the strength of conviction regarding the existence of life after death;
the importance placed on religion.

The measure of Christian fundamentalist belief is also based on three measures:[6]

the strength of conviction about the existence of a devil;
whether or not the individual described himself/herself as a "Born Again Christian";
beliefs regarding the importance of Christ for salvation.

The two measures of the orthodoxy of religious belief are themselves fairly highly correlated ($r = .52$). By either measure, Christian orthodoxy is most widespread among non-Jews who are:

Table 8.5. Religious Conviction, Christian Fundamentalism, and Anti-Semitism among Non-Jews

		Anti-Semitism index		
		Prejudiced (%)	Neutral (%)	Unprejudiced (%)
Total non-Jews	(100%)	23	32	45
Religious conviction				
High	(100%)	25	37	39
Medium	(100%)	25	31	44
Low	(100%)	19	24	58
Christian fundamentalism				
High	(100%)	25	36	39
Medium	(100%)	24	32	44
Non-fundamentalist	(100%)	18	25	57

older;
nonwhite;
less educated;
from rural areas;
Baptists.

Clearly, then, Christian orthodoxy is most commonly found in those groups that are likely to exhibit the highest levels of anti-Semitism. For example, nearly one out of two (46 percent) individuals who have not graduated from high school are high in fundamentalist belief compared to one in four (25 percent) college graduates and postgraduates.

It should come as no surprise, therefore, that an analysis of the relationship between Christian orthodoxy and anti-Semitism reveals that both measures of religious belief are significantly correlated with anti-Semitism. Among non-Jews who exhibit a high score on the religious conviction index, 38 percent are unprejudiced compared to 57 percent of those who exhibit a low level of religious conviction. Similarly, 39 percent of those who are high in Christian fundamentalism are unprejudiced compared to 57 percent of those who are non-fundamentalists.

The current study indicates, however, that the relationship between Christian orthodoxy and anti-Semitism is due almost entirely to three demographic factors: education, race, and age. For example, the correlation between religious conviction and anti-Semitism is .11, indicating that there is a small but significant positive relationship—individuals who are characterized by greater religious conviction are somewhat more likely to be anti-Semitic. However, after controlling for education, race, and age, we find that the partial correlation between religiousness and anti-Semitism virtually disappears, indicating that the apparent relationship is actually due to the fact that individuals who are traditional in their religious outlook are more likely to be older, less educated, and black—all factors that are associated with higher levels of anti-Semitic belief.

Table 8.6. Correlation of Christian Orthodoxy and Anti-Semitism among Non-Jews

	Correlation with anti-Semitism (%)	Partial correlation controlling for:		
		Education (%)	Education and race (%)	Education, race and age (%)
Religious conviction	.11	.07	.06	.04
Christian fundamentalist	.10	.06	.02	.01

It is the effects of these related background factors, then, and not the effect of religious beliefs themselves, that produce a higher level of anti-Semitism among those with orthodox Christian religious beliefs.

SUMMARY

Over the past 15 years, Christian orthodoxy and religious affiliation have been among the most frequently researched and discussed correlates of anti-Semitism. The current analysis reveals three major themes of the "religious factor."

First, religion has become in many ways a less significant factor in life in the United States during the past 20 years. More specifically, Christian orthodoxy has declined significantly since 1964. For example, one out of two (50 percent) Americans described religion as "extremely important" in 1964; today that figure is under four out of ten (38 percent).

Second, despite the decline, Christian orthodoxy continues to be somewhat related to anti-Semitism. For example, one in four (25 percent) Christian fundamentalists are prejudiced compared to one in five (19 percent) nonfundamentalists.

Third, the association of religion and anti-Semitism is, however, due to the effects of age, education, and race. After we control for these three demographic factors, the association of both religious conviction and Christian fundamentalism with anti-Semitism disappears.

NOTES

1. Gallup Organization, *Religion in America* (Princeton: The Gallup Organization and the Princeton Religion Research Center, Inc., 1981).
2. D. Yankelovich, "Stepchildren of the Moral Majority," *Psychology Today,* November 1981, p. 5.
3. Harold Quinley and Charles Glock, *Anti-Semitism in America* (New York: Harper & Row, 1979), p. 109.
4. G. Selznick and S. Steinberg, *The Tenacity of Prejudice* (New York: Harper & Row, 1969); C. Glock and R. Stark, *Christian Beliefs and Anti-Semitism* (New York: Harper & Row, 1966); R. Stark et al., *Wayward Shepherds: Prejudice and the Protestant Clergy* (New York: Harper & Row, 1971); R. Middleton, "Do Christian Beliefs Cause Anti-Semitism?" *American Sociological Review* 38 (1973): 33–52; W. C. Roof, "Religious Orthodoxy and Minority Prejudice: Causal Relationship or Reflection of Localistic World View?" *American Journal of Sociology* 80 (1974): 643–664.
5. See questions 25, 29, and 30 in questionnaire (Appendix D) for exact wording.
6. See questions 26, 27a, and 28 in questionnaire (Appendix D) for exact wording.

9

ATTITUDES TOWARD ISRAEL AND
ATTITUDES TOWARD AMERICAN JEWS

Since the research for *The Tenacity of Prejudice* was conducted in 1964, the role of Israel on the world's stage has changed dramatically. Israel and its relations with its Arab neighbors have come to occupy a critical position in geopolitics. This change has come about for two reasons. First, the Arab-Israeli wars in 1967 and 1973 placed the Middle East at center stage; and second, and perhaps more important, the increase in Arab influence due to OPEC has made Arab-Israeli relations a crucial factor in world energy supplies and, indeed, in the global economy. The increasing knowledge and concern regarding Arab-Israeli difficulties is reflected in the fact that, in response to the Gallup Poll in June 1967, only 59 percent of Americans said that they were aware of or knew something about the troubles between Israel and the Arab nations. Knowledge of this conflict now is nearly universal.

Because of the increasing significance of Israel for the United States and other western nations, the current study focuses on American attitudes toward Israel and their impact on attitudes toward American Jews.

The analysis in this chapter will proceed in three steps. First, attitudes toward Israel, and in particular a number of trends in attitudes since 1977, are examined. The 1977 data were also gathered for the American Jewish Committee by Yankelovich, Skelly and White, Inc. Second, attitudes of Jews and non-Jews toward Israel are compared. Third, the relationship between attitudes toward Israel and attitudes toward American Jews is examined.

It is important to point out that the data in the current study were gathered in early 1981. A good deal has happened in the Middle East since that time, including Israel's relinquishing of the remainder of Sinai, Israeli bombing of Lebanon, and a general strike throughout the Arab world in support of the Palestinian cause.

Consequently, the data that follow may be somewhat different from an up-to-the-minute reading of public attitudes.

ATTITUDES TOWARD ISRAEL

U.S. support for Israel remains quite solid. The majority of Americans and a substantial majority of those with an opinion hold quite favorable views. Nevertheless, since 1977, there are some signs of erosion in that support, though it is important to add that there has been no growth in support for the Arab cause. The basic trend in

Table 9.1. Attitudes toward Israel among All Respondents

	1977 (%)	1981 (%)
The United States should		
Increase military aid to Israel	10	10
Continue military aid at same level	49	47
Cut back on military aid	26	23
Not sure	15	20
Continuation of (U.S.) support for Israel is		
Very important	n.a.[a]	23
Somewhat important	n.a.	46
Not at all important	n.a.	18
Not sure	n.a.	13
The continuation of Israel as a Jewish state is		
Important	61	51
Not important	21	25
Not sure	18	24
Think Israel has the right to make Jerusalem its capital		
Yes	n.a.	48
No	n.a.	17
Not sure	n.a.	35

[a]Trend measurement not available.

attitudes since 1977 has been a growth in uncertainty about the situation in the Middle East.

United States' Support For Israel

Americans' attitudes toward U.S. support for Israel remain quite firm. Two out of three (67 percent) Americans feel that it is very important or somewhat important that "we continue to support Israel," and few (18 percent) believe that it is "not at all important." This general endorsement is more than mere lip service. Indeed, it extends to the provision of military aid as well. Six out of ten (59 percent) Americans believe that U.S. military aid to Israel should be increased or continue at current levels. This support level has remained essentially unchanged since 1977, when it was 57 percent. One interesting aspect of it is that it appears to be nonpartisan, extending to all major groups regardless of their political outlook, region of the country, or background characteristics such as age, education, or religion.

Israel's Political Sovereignty

The majority (51 percent) of Americans and more than three out of four with an opinion continue to believe that the continuation of Israel as a Jewish state is important to themselves and to the United States. Despite the widespread agreement with Israel's right to exist as a Jewish state, there has been some lessening in support for this concept since 1977, when 61 percent said that Israel's existence as a Jewish state was important to themselves and to the nation.

In a separate but related area, one out of two (48 percent) Americans say they believe that Israel has the right to make Jerusalem its capital, while 17 percent say it does not have that right and 35 percent are not sure. Unlike support for military aid to Israel, the question of Jerusalem as the capital is highly related to age and education. The young and better-educated are considerably more likely to have an opinion on the issue and are generally quite supportive of Israel's right. For example, among young people between the ages of 18 and 29, 60 percent believe Israel has the right to make Jerusalem its capital compared to 17 percent who do not.

Attitudes toward Israel versus the Arab Nations

Despite the growing economic power of the Arab nations, there has been no indication in recent years of growing popular support for the Arab cause. In 1977, 2 percent of all Americans said that, if there were a war between the Arab countries and Israel, they would sympathize with the Arabs. Five years later, that figure is essentially unchanged (3 percent). In contrast, more than four out of ten Americans said they would sympathize with Israel in 1977 and again in 1981.

Despite the fact that American sympathies have remained decidedly with the Israelis rather than the Arabs, there has been a significant change in one area of American attitudes toward Arab-Israeli relations: that is, the Palestinian issue. In 1977, 40 percent of Americans and a substantial majority of those with an opinion said they believed Israel was doing "the right thing in refusing to negotiate with the PLO." By 1981 there had been a dramatic change of opinion in this area. In the spring of 1981, 26 percent of Americans said that refusing to negotiate with the PLO was "the right thing" compared to 31 percent who said it was "the wrong thing." This sentiment represented a reversal of opinion from a plurality opposing to a plurality favoring negotiation with the PLO.

In the same direction, though less extreme, are changing attitudes toward a Palestinian state on the West Bank. In 1977, 37 percent of Americans said they thought Israel's position on a Palestinian state was reasonable compared to 28 percent who viewed it as unreasonable. By 1981, the proportion of Americans who regarded Israeli opposition to a Palestinian state on the West Bank as reasonable dropped from 37 percent to 31 percent.

American Attitudes toward the Treatment of Arabs in Israel

There has been no change since 1964 in the level of American awareness of the relationship between Jews and Arabs in Israel. However, among individuals who are aware, there is now a more favorable attitude toward the treatment of the Arabs in Israel. In 1964, 26 percent of Americans thought Arabs in Israel were treated well, compared to four out of ten (43 percent) who thought they were treated badly. In 1981, the opposite pattern held: four out of ten (43 per-

Table 9.2. Trends in Attitudes toward Relations of Israel and the
Arabs among All Respondents

	1977 (%)	1981 (%)
If there were a war between the Arab nations and Israel, would you sympathize with		
Israel	45	46
Arabs	2	3
Neither	41	27
Not sure	12	24
Is Israel doing the right thing or the wrong thing in refusing to negotiate with the PLO?		
Right thing	40	26
Wrong thing	21	31
Not sure	39	43
Israeli attitudes toward a Palestinian state on the West Bank are		
Reasonable	37	31
Unreasonable	28	27
Not sure	35	42
	1964 (%)	1981 (%)
Aware of relations between Jews and Arabs in Israel		
Yes	35	34
No	62	66
Not sure	3	—[a]
Believe Arabs in Israel are treated[b]		
Very well	5	7
Pretty well	21	37
Pretty badly	34	27
Very badly	9	8
Not sure	31	21

[a]Less than 0.5%.
[b]Based on those who are aware of relations between Jews and Arabs in Israel.

cent) believed the Arabs in Israel were treated well and one in three (35 percent) believed they were treated badly.

Index of Attitudes toward Israel

Through the use of factor analysis[1] a four-item index of attitudes was developed as a means of obtaining a general profile of the demographic and nondemographic factors associated with attitudes toward Israel. The index consists of the following four items:

Continuation of Israel as a Jewish state is important/not important.
It is very/somewhat/not that important that we continue to support Israel.
United States should increase/continue/reduce military aid to Israel.
Would sympathize with Israel/Arab nations in the Mid East war.

The analysis of the distribution of scores indicates that, through the use of the index, we can characterize 32 percent of Americans as highly favorable in their attitudes toward Israel, 41 percent as somewhat favorable and 27 percent as critical. The legitimacy of these descriptive labels can be seen by examining the cross tabulation of

Table 9.3. Attitudes toward Israel by Its Constituent Items among All Respondents

| | | Attitudes toward Israel | | |
	Total (%)	Highly favorable (32%) (%)	Somewhat favorable (41%) (%)	Critical (27%) (%)
Continuation of Israel as a Jewish state is important.	51	94	47	6
It is very/somewhat important that we continue to support Israel.	68	96	67	38
United States should increase/ continue military aid to Israel.	57	90	51	29
I would sympathize with Israel in Middle East war.	45	88	31	15

the index with its constituent items. The highly favorable are consistently nearly universally supportive of Israel. The somewhat favorable are much like the general public as a whole in their outlook and tend to be more favorable than not. The critical tend to express little support for Israel.

Figure 9.1. Attitudes toward Israel among Non-Jews

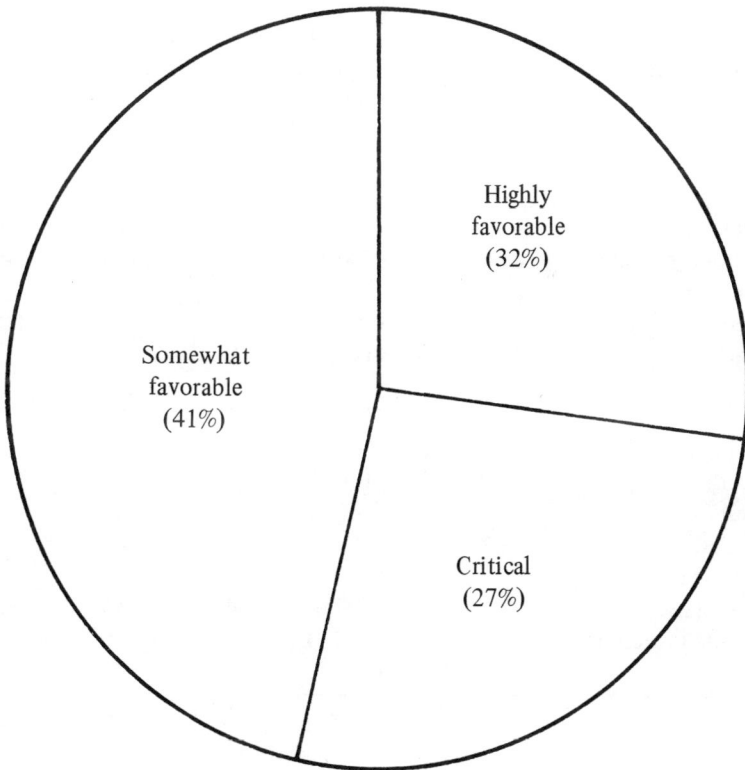

Profile of Attitudes Toward Israel

Perhaps the most important finding of the analysis of the profile of attitudes toward Israel is that the vast majority of members of every demographic group are highly or somewhat favorable in their attitude. The group most critical of Israel is blacks. However, even here, the majority (65 percent) are highly or somewhat favorable and

Table 9.4. Profile of Attitudes toward Israel among All Respondents

		Attitudes toward Israel		
		Highly favorable (%)	Somewhat favorable (%)	Unfavorable (%)
Total	(100%)	32	41	27
Age				
18–29 years	(100%)	38	33	29
30–39 years	(100%)	31	40	29
40–55 years	(100%)	36	41	23
55 years and over	(100%)	34	43	23
Education				
Did not graduate from high school	(100%)	25	43	32
High school graduate	(100%)	29	42	29
Some college	(100%)	41	39	20
College graduate/postgraduate	(100%)	45	34	21
Race				
White	(100%)	35	40	25
Black	(100%)	20	45	35
Region				
Northeast	(100%)	31	39	30
Midwest	(100%)	32	40	28
South	(100%)	36	41	23
West	(100%)	29	44	27
Religion				
Catholic	(100%)	28	44	28
Protestant	(100%)	34	40	26
White Protestant	(100%)	36	40	24
Jewish	(100%)	92	4	4

(Table continued on page 85.)

only 35 percent are critical. Attitudes toward Israel are related to a number of other demographic, social, and political factors in addition to race.

Education

Better-educated Americans are considerably more supportive of Israel than are the less educated. For example, 45 percent of college

Table 9.4, continued

		Attitudes toward Israel		
		Highly favorable (%)	Somewhat favorable (%)	Unfavor-able (%)
Sex				
Male	(100%)	35	38	27
Female	(100%)	30	44	26
Political outlook				
Conservative	(100%)	37	37	26
Moderate	(100%)	30	44	26
Liberal	(100%)	31	42	27
Vote in 1980 election				
Carter	(100%)	30	44	26
Reagan	(100%)	43	36	21
Respondent's occupation				
Professional/executive		44	37	19
Other white collar		32	44	24
Blue collar		30	41	29
Retired		30	41	29
Housewife		29	42	29
Political party affiliation				
Democrat		31	42	27
Republican		38	36	26
Independent		40	39	21
Type of area				
Central city		33	41	26
Suburb		38	36	26
Rural/small town		26	44	30

graduates are highly favorable compared to 25 percent of those who have not graduated from high school.

Political Outlook

Conservatives tend to be slightly more favorable toward Israel than moderates or liberals. Also, Independents, Republicans, and individuals who voted for Reagan in the 1980 election are somewhat more likely to be favorable toward Israel than are Democrats and Carter supporters.

Sex

Men are somewhat more likely to be supportive of Israel than women.

Type of Area

Individuals living in suburban areas and to a lesser extent those in central cities are more likely to be favorable toward Israel than those in small towns and rural areas.

Trends in Attitudes toward Jewish Loyalty to Israel

In Chapter 3 it was reported that, since 1964, there has been an increase in the proportion of Americans who believe that Jews are more loyal to Israel than to the United States. This erosion in the level of loyalty that Jews are perceived to feel toward the United States is confirmed again in comparisons with the 1977 Yankelovich study. In 1977, one out of two (50 percent) Americans said they believed "Jews feel closer to the United States than to Israel." By 1981, that figure had dropped to 41 percent. Similarly, in 1977, 45 percent of Americans said that if the United States and Israel ever

Table 9.5. Trends in Attitudes toward Loyalty of Jews in the United States among All Respondents

	1977 (%)	1981 (%)
Believe American Jews feel closer to		
The United States	50	41
Israel	27	27
Both	10	8
Neither	13	24
If the United States and Israel ever broke off relations, most American Jews would side with		
The United States	45	35
Israel	31	31
Both	8	6
Not sure	16	28

broke off relations, most American Jews would side with the United States. By 1981, that figure had fallen to 35 percent. There is clear evidence then, of increased uncertainty in the minds of many Americans regarding Jewish-American loyalty to the United States versus Israel.

Attitudes toward Israel: Jews versus Non-Jews

Not surprisingly, American Jews are nearly universally supportive of Israel. Nine out of ten (93 percent) say that the continuation of Israel as a Jewish state is important to themselves and to the nation. Similarly, eight out of ten (83 percent) say that continued United States support for Israel is very important. When it comes to military aid, there is, again, widespread support among American Jews. One out of two (48 percent) believe that military aid to Israel should be increased compared to one in ten (9 percent) non-Jews. Also, only 2 percent of American Jews feel military aid to Israel should be cut back.

Table 9.6. Attitudes toward Israel: Jews versus Non-Jews

	Non-Jews (%)	Jews (%)
The United States should		
Increase military aid to Israel	9	48
Continue military aid at same level	47	45
Cut back on military aid	23	2
Not sure	21	5
The continuation of (U.S.) support for Israel is		
Very important	21	83
Somewhat important	46	12
Not at all important	19	2
Not sure	14	3
The continuation of Israel as a Jewish state is		
Important	50	93
Not important	26	5
Not sure	24	2
Think Israel has the right to make Jerusalem its capital		
Yes	48	74
No	17	14
Not sure	35	12

Table 9.7. Attitudes toward Relations of Israel and the Arab Nations: Jews versus Non-Jews

	Non-Jews (%)	Jews (%)
If there were a war between the Arab nations and Israel, would you sympathize with		
Israel	44	95
Arabs	3	–
Neither	28	2
Not sure	25	3
Is Israel doing the right thing or the wrong thing in refusing to negotiate with the PLO?		
Right thing	25	62
Wrong thing	31	28
Not sure	44	10
Israeli attitudes toward a Palestinian state on the West Bank are		
Reasonable	30	71
Unreasonable	27	17
Not sure	43	12
Attitude toward Israel's refusal to give back Golan Heights		
Reasonable	n.a.[a]	78
Unreasonable	n.a.	13
Not sure	n.a.	9
Aware of relations between Jews and Arabs in Israel		
Yes	34	62
No	66	38
Not sure		
Believe Arabs in Israel are treated[b]		
Very well	6	27
Pretty well	37	42
Pretty badly	27	15
Very badly	8	8
Not sure	22	8

[a]Trend data not available.
[b]Based on those who are aware of relations between Arabs and Jews in Israel.

One issue where there is less than complete consensus for the Israeli position among American Jews is that of Jerusalem. While three out of four (74 percent) Jews believe that Israel does have the right to make Jerusalem its capital, 14 percent do not and 12 percent say they are not sure.

Attitudes toward Arab-Israeli Relations

Obviously, support for the Arab cause among American Jews is virtually nonexistent in the general population (though it is, of course, not unheard of in Jewish intellectual circles).

Consistent with this near universal support for Israel's position vis-à-vis the Arab nations, Israel's position regarding the PLO and a Palestinian state also draws widespread support among American Jews. Six out of ten (62 percent) believe that Israel is doing the right thing in refusing to negotiate with the PLO, and seven out of ten agree that Israel is being reasonable in opposing a Palestinian state on the West Bank of the Jordan River. Nevertheless, as these numbers make clear, even among American Jews support for the Israeli position regarding the Palestinians is not universally accepted. Indeed, a sizeable minority (28 percent) did not believe in early 1981 that Israel "is doing the right thing" in refusing to negotiate with the PLO.

ISRAELI TREATMENT OF ARABS IN ISRAEL

Given the greater salience of Israel for American Jews, it should come as no surprise that nearly two out of three (62 percent) American Jews say they are aware of the treatment of Arabs in Israel, compared to one out of three (34 percent) non-Jews. Jews are also more likely to believe that Arabs in Israel are treated well. Overall, 69 percent of American Jews say that Arabs in Israel are treated very well or pretty well, compared to one in four (23 percent) who believe the Arabs in Israel are treated pretty badly or very badly.

Attitudes Toward Jewish Loyalty

Jews are more likely than non-Jews to reject the idea that American Jews are more loyal to Israel than to the United States. Just over

Table 9.8. Attitudes toward Loyalty of Jews in the
United States: Jews versus Non-Jews among All Respondents

	Non-Jews (%)	Jews (%)
Believe American Jews feel closer to		
The United States	41	70
Israel	27	7
Both	8	18
Neither	24	5
If the United States and Israel ever broke off relations, most American Jews would side with		
The United States	35	43
Israel	31	26
Both	6	14
Not sure	28	17

one in four (27 percent) non-Jews say they believe American Jews feel closer to Israel than to the United States compared to fewer than one in ten (7 percent) Jews. Nevertheless, it is clear that the issue of dual loyalty is grounded in more than simply anti-Semitic prejudice. Indeed, when Jews were asked who they felt most American Jews would side with if the United States and Israel ever broke off relations, 43 percent said the United States and 26 percent said Israel, indicating that many American Jews are conscious of the issue of dual loyalty.

ANTI-SEMITISM AND ATTITUDES TOWARD ISRAEL

There is a clear association between attitudes toward American Jews and attitudes toward Israel. For example, compared to those who are prejudiced, those who are unprejudiced are more likely to: favor continued military support for Israel; believe that the continuation of Israel is important; think Israel has the right to make Jerusalem its capital; and believe Arabs in Israel are well treated.

Despite this association, it is important to note that support for Israel is so pervasive in American society that it transcends negative attitudes toward Jews. For example, even among those who are prejudiced, a majority favor a continuation or increase in military aid to Israel and only 29 percent favor a cutback. Similarly 60 percent of the prejudiced believe that it is very important or somewhat important that the United States continue to support Israel.

There is little indication of support for the Arab cause among those who are prejudiced, though it is important to note that many non-Jews who are prejudiced say that, in an Arab-Israeli war, they would support neither side (33 percent) or are not sure (24 percent).

Prejudice against American Jews does not appear to be strongly tied to a rejection of support for Israel nor to Israel's right to exist. However, one aspect of relations between the United States and

Table 9.9. The Anti-Semitism Index and Attitudes toward Israel

		Anti-Semitism index		
	Total (%)	Unprejudiced (%)	Neutral (%)	Prejudiced (%)
The United States should				
Increase military aid to Israel	10	11	8	7
Continue military aid at same level	47	53	43	44
Cut back on military aid	23	24	17	29
Not sure	20	12	32	20
Continuation of (U.S.) support for Israel is				
Very important	23	25	17	18
Somewhat important	46	51	44	42
Not at all important	18	14	17	30
Not sure	13	10	22	10
The continuation of Israel as a Jewish state is				
Important	51	56	40	47
Not important	25	28	21	30
Not sure	24	16	39	23
Think Israel has the right to make Jerusalem its capital				
Yes	48	52	42	45
No	17	22	11	16
Not sure	35	26	47	39

Table 9.10. The Anti-Semitism Index and Attitudes toward Relations of Israel and the Arabs

	Total (%)	Anti-Semitism index		
		Unprejudiced (%)	Neutral (%)	Prejudiced (%)
If there were a war between the Arab nations and Israel would you sympathize with				
Israel	46	52	34	35
Arabs	3	2	2	8
Neither	27	26	31	33
Not sure	24	20	33	24
Is Israel doing the right thing or the wrong thing in refusing to negotiate with the PLO?				
Right thing	26	29	19	24
Wrong thing	31	40	15	37
Not sure	43	31	66	39
Israeli attitudes toward a Palestinian state on the West Bank are				
Reasonable	31	35	25	27
Unreasonable	27	35	13	31
Not sure	42	30	62	42
Aware of relations between Jews and Arabs in Israel				
Yes	34	39	24	35
No	66	61	76	65
Believe Arabs in Israel are treated[a]				
Very well	7	6	5	7
Pretty well	37	43	28	31
Pretty badly	27	28	31	21
Very badly	8	7	6	13
Not sure	21	16	30	28

[a]Based on those who are aware of relations between Jews and Arabs in Israel.

Israel is relevant to anti-Semitic prejudice, and that is the dual loyalty issue. For example, among the unprejudiced a plurality believe that most American Jews would side with the United States if Israel and the United States ever broke off relations. Among the prejudiced however, a plurality believe that most American Jews would side with Israel. The criticism here, of course, is not necessarily of Israel, but of American Jews.

Table 9.11. The Anti-Semitism Index and Attitudes toward Loyalty of Jews in the United States

	Total (%)	Unprejudiced (%)	Neutral (%)	Prejudiced (%)
Believe American Jews feel closer to				
The United States	41	55	29	29
Israel	27	22	23	44
Both	8	7	7	10
Neither	24	16	41	17
If the United States and Israel ever broke off relations, most American Jews would side with				
The United States	35	44	27	27
Israel	31	30	24	42
Both	6	6	4	8
Not sure	28	20	45	23

Perhaps the clearest summary of the relationship between attitudes toward Israel and those toward American Jews is provided by the crosstabulation of the indexes measuring these two phenomena. One in three (32 percent) individuals who have a critical view of Israel are prejudiced compared to one in five (21 percent) who are highly favorable. Looking at it in reverse, we find that, even among those who are prejudiced in their attitudes toward Jews, a majority (60 percent) are highly or somewhat favorable in their attitudes toward Israel.

The relatively limited impact of attitudes toward Israel on negative attitudes toward American Jews is also supported by the fact

Table 9.12. Attitudes toward Israel and the Anti-Semitism Index

| | Total (%) | Attitudes toward Israel | | |
		Highly favorable (%)	Somewhat favorable (%)	Critical (%)
Total	100	100	100	100
	100	32	41	27
Anti-Semitism index				
Prejudiced	23	21	17	32
	100	27	33	40
Neutral	32	25	38	30
	100	24	50	26
Unprejudiced	45	54	45	38
	100	37	41	22

Note: Top number in each cell is vertically percentaged, and bottom number is horizontally percentaged.

that, when asked a direct question about it, the vast majority of non-Jews say that the existence of Israel has not affected their attitude toward American Jews. Among those who say their views have been affected, 6 percent say they think more highly and 4 percent say they think less highly of American Jews. There is little indication, therefore, that Israel and its policies have had a significant adverse impact on attitudes toward American Jews.

It is interesting to note, however, that Jews themselves say they have been affected. Six out of ten (60 percent) American Jews say that the existence of Israel has made them more proud of being Jewish, and few say it has made them less proud.

Summary

Support for Israel remains quite strong despite some erosion, and there has been no growth in support for the Arab cause between 1977 and 1981.

One out of two Americans and two out of three with an opinion believe the continuation of Israel is important to people like themselves.

The majority of Americans and seven out of ten with an opinion believe that U.S. military aid to Israel should be increased or continue at the same level.

Virtually no Americans would sympathize with the Arabs in an Arab-Israeli war.

Despite this fundamentally strong support, there was a growing belief among Americans in early 1981 that Israel is doing the wrong thing in refusing to negotiate with the PLO. This concern may be at the heart of the erosion of support for Israel that has taken place since 1977. This erosion has not directly benefited the Arab cause but rather manifests itself in the increasing proportion of Americans who are not sure how they feel about U.S. policy toward Israel.

Generally speaking, support for Israel is most widespread among college graduates, Reagan supporters, conservatives, whites, and males.

Overall, there is a significant association between negative attitudes toward Israel and negative attitudes toward American Jews. However, because of the generally favorable attitudes toward Israel, there is little evidence that these have had a negative impact on attitudes toward American Jews. In fact even among individuals who can be described as critical of Israel, only one in three (33 percent) are prejudiced.

NOTE

1. See Appendix C for factor loadings.

10

DIFFERENCES IN THE BACKGROUNDS, BELIEFS, AND EXPERIENCES OF JEWS AND NON-JEWS

Much of the current study focuses on Americans' perceptions regarding differences between Jews and non-Jews. In contrast, this chapter examines actual differences between Jewish and non-Jewish respondents in terms of their background characteristics, attitudes, and values, and the relationship between these real differences and the perception of differences.

Since they constitute between 2 and 3 percent of all adults in the United States, opinion surveys rarely have reliable samples of Jews. To compensate for the small proportion in the United States' population, the current study made use of a large oversample of Jews. In all, 174 interviews were conducted with Jewish respondents.[1]

DEMOGRAPHIC DIFFERENCES

The demographic portrait of Jews that emerges from this study is a familiar one. Compared to non-Jews, they are more likely to be affluent, college educated, employed in white-collar occupations, live in the Northeast, and have grown up in a "big city."

The economic and occupational success of Jews is, of course, widely recognized by non-Jews. Indeed the majority (56 percent) of non-Jews believe that "Jews have more money than most people" and few (1 percent) non-Jews believe that Jews have less money. While it is rooted in real differences between Jews and non-Jews, this appraisal of the economic success of Jews is nevertheless related to

Table 10.1. Demographic Profile of Jews versus Non-Jews

	Total (%)	Non-Jews (%)	Jews (%)
Sex			
Men	47	47	45
Women	53	53	55
Age			
18–29 years	28	29	20
30–39 years	22	21	24
40–54 years	22	22	24
55 years and over	28	28	32
Education			
Did not graduate from high school	29	29	12
High school graduate	36	37	21
Some college	18	18	29
College graduate	17	16	38
Respondent's occupation			
Professional/executive/owner	18	17	36
White collar	15	15	26
Blue collar	32	33	7
Retired	9	9	10
Housewife	18	18	14
Other	8	8	7
Region			
Northeast	23	22	68
Midwest	26	27	12
South	33	33	13
West	18	18	7
City size			
1 million or more	9	8	37
250,000–999,999	10	10	2
100,000–249,999	13	13	7
50,000–99,999	9	9	14
25,000–49,999	7	7	12
10,000–24,999	13	13	12
Less than 9,999	31	32	9
Unincorporated suburb	8	8	7
Type of place grew up			
Big city	18	17	62
Suburb of big city	12	11	12
Medium-size city	18	18	10
Small city	6	6	2
Small town	27	28	14
Farm	19	19	0
No answer		1	0
Family income[a]			
Under $15,000	37	38	25
$15,000–24,999	28	30	15
$25,000–34,999	20	19	30
$35,000 and over	15	13	30

[a]Based on those answering.

Table 10.2. Anti-Semitism and the Perception of Jewish Wealth among Non-Jews

| | Total non-Jews (%) | Believe Jews have more money than most people (56%) | | | Believe Jews have same amount of money as others (32%) (%) |
		Total (%)	And are bothered by this belief (7%) (%)	And are not bothered by this belief (40%) (%)	
Anti-Semitism index					
Prejudiced	23	32	54	28	11
Neutral	31	26	18	27	29
Unprejudiced	46	42	28	45	60

anti-Semitic beliefs. One in ten (13 percent) non-Jews who believe "Jews have more money than most people" explicitly say that they are bothered by this belief and the remainder do not.

We have, then, three different perceptions about Jewish affluence. The first group, constituting 7 percent of all non-Jews, say that they believe Jews have "more money than most people" and they are "bothered by this belief." The second group, constituting 40 percent of all non-Jews, is made up of those who say that Jews have more money than most people and that they are "not bothered by this belief"; the final group is made up of those non-Jews who believe that Jews have "the same amount of money" as other people (32 percent). It is interesting and indeed important to note that there is a direct relationship between perceptions of Jewish wealth and prejudice. The majority of those who believe Jews have more money than most people and are "bothered" by this belief are prejudiced. Among those who accept this belief about Jewish wealth but say they are not bothered by it, the level of anti-Semitic prejudice falls to 28 percent. However it is significantly higher than the 11 percent who are prejudiced among those who believe Jews are not wealthier than most people.

There are two important lessons here: first is the fact that perceptions of Jewish wealth are tied to anti-Semitism in general; and second, and perhaps more important, is the limitation of self reports. Despite their denials about being bothered about their perception of Jewish wealth, non-Jews who accept this belief are more likely to be prejudiced.

RELIGIOUS BELIEFS AND PRACTICES

The religious identity of Jews is quite varied. One out of three (33 percent) describe themselves as Conservative, one in five (19 percent) as Reform, one in ten (10 percent) as Orthodox, and the largest number—nearly four out of ten (38 percent)—describe themselves as being "just Jewish." Overall, one out of two (52 percent) Jews say they are affiliated with a synagogue.

Table 10.3. Religious Beliefs and Practices of Jews and Non-Jews

	Total (%)	Non-Jews (%)	Jews (%)
Know God really exists and I have no doubts about it	62	63	38
Regard religion as "extremely important" or "quite important"	64	64	43
Attend religious services "every week" or "nearly every week"	43	43	14

Unlike the issue of wealth, where there is some correspondence between the perception of non-Jews and the facts of Jewish life, when it comes to religion, non-Jews' images of Jews do not appear to reflect reality. The vast majority (71 percent) of non-Jews believe that Jews are highly religious. However, there are a variety of indications in the current study that, in terms of both religious beliefs and ritual observance, Jews are less religious than non-Jews. For example, 63 percent of non-Jews agree that "I know God really exists and I have no doubts about it" compared to 38 percent of Jews. Similarly, 43 percent of non-Jews say they attend religious services every week or nearly every week, compared to 14 percent of Jews. Also, Jews are significantly less likely than non-Jews to say they regard religion as "extremely important" or "quite important."

The relatively weak ties to traditional ritual observance may also be one important factor in explaining why 69 percent of Jews who were interviewed said that they felt Jews "were losing their distinctive identity." Though it is important to point out in this context that, while Jews are somewhat less likely than non-Jews to describe religion as very important, nevertheless nine out of ten Jews or more say that Chanukah, Passover, Rosh Hashana, and Yom Kippur are important to them personally.

SOCIAL VALUES

When it comes to the importance they place on the major spheres of social life, by and large Jews and non-Jews share quite similar views. They are likely to place roughly equal emphasis on critical spheres of life such as friendship, family, work, and money. Contrary to traditional stereotypes and indeed to sociological theories that explain the economic success of Jews as the product of a "love of education," the current study indicates that, while they are indeed better educated, Jews are no more likely than non-Jews to say they regard education as very important. In fact, blacks are slightly more likely to say they value education than are Jews or other whites.

Consistently with the previous discussion of religion, Jews are less likely to describe religion as "very important." Also, they are less likely to view patriotism and "living a clean moral life as important." However, acceptance of each of these traditional values is highly related to education. For example, individuals with lower levels of education are more likely to regard patriotism and religion as important values. The lower level of emphasis placed on these traditional values by Jews is, therefore, a consequence of higher educational level rather than the direct effect of religious differences.

POLITICAL OUTLOOK AND BEHAVIOR

In the area of political attitudes and values there are important similarities as well as important differences in the outlook of Jews and non-Jews. While Jews are more likely than non-Jews to be moderate to liberal in political outlook and Democratic in party affiliation, in many ways their political views are nevertheless quite similar

Table 10.4. Political and Economic Issues and Concerns
among All Respondents

	Total (%)	Non-Jews (%)	Jews (%)
Very important			
Strong national defense	82	82	79
A federal tax cut	56	56	50
Freedom of speech	88	89	93
Freedom of the press	75	75	91
Federal job programs for the inner cities	37	37	35
A strong U.S. economy	91	91	93
Reducing air and water pollution	68	68	71
Providing aid for developing nations	18	18	24
Increasing racial equality	43	42	53
Increasing equality for women	54	54	62
Separation of church and state	57	57	79
Reducing U.S. dependence on other nations	73	73	74
Worried a lot about			
Losing your job because of the economy	27	27	22
A recession	50	50	57
An energy shortage	51	51	66
Another war in the Middle East	47	47	61
The possibility of a world war	47	47	48

to those of non-Jews. For example, Jews and non-Jews express quite similar views regarding the importance of a strong national defense, job programs for the inner cities, and reducing air and water pollution. Also, Jews are as likely as non-Jews to say they have grown more conservative in recent years.

Despite certain political views that are shared by Jews and non-Jews, there are also significant differences. Domestically, the political view of Jews can be characterized as generally more supportive of civil liberties issues; for example, Jews are more likely to be concerned about equality for minorities and women. They are more likely to support the right of an atheist to hold office or teach in a public high school. And they are more likely to express support for the separation of church and state.

One area of church-state relations that is of particular concern to Jews is prayer in school. Overall, 65 percent of all Jews say they are opposed and 48 percent say they are strongly opposed to prayer in school. In contrast, only one in five (21 percent) non-Jews oppose prayer in public school.

The reason for Jewish support for constitutionally guaranteed civil rights is quite clear and well grounded in their experience as a minority with a long history of oppression, frequently with the complicity, if not the outright sanction of the prevailing legal system.

If greater emphasis on civil rights is the chief factor that appears to distinguish the domestic political views of Jews and non-Jews, when it comes to international political concerns, the main difference between them is their attitudes toward Israel. While we have dealt with the question of Israel at length in Chapter 9, it is worth noting here that Jews are significantly more concerned than non-Jews about an energy shortage and war in the Middle East despite the fact that they are more affluent and no more concerned about the possibility of war in general. It is clear that the source of this Jewish anxiety is the great concern and pride that American Jews feel regarding Israel.

MOOD OF THE NATION AND CONFIDENCE IN THE FUTURE

Another area of real similarity between Jews and non-Jews is feelings about the state of the nation. In early 1981, both Jews and non-Jews were quite pessimistic. Only one in three members of each group felt things were going very well in the country, while two out of three said they believed things were going very badly or pretty badly. Similarly, one in four Jews and non-Jews felt that the nation's "problems are no worse than at other times," while just under seven out of ten believe "the country is in deep and serious trouble."

While both Jews and non-Jews shared a sense of pessimism about the state of the nation, members of both groups also expressed a good deal of confidence about the country's future prosperity. Taken together, more than eight out of ten Jews and non-Jews said that they had a lot of confidence or some confidence that the nation's future would be strong and prosperous.

SUMMARY

There are important similarities and differences between Jews and non-Jews in their background and beliefs. In terms of socioeconomic characteristics, Jews are clearly better educated, more affluent, and more likely to be found in white-collar occupations than are non-Jews. While they are quite different in many of their demographic characteristics, in terms of their basic social values, Jews are quite similar to non-Jews. They place equal emphasis on such things as family, education, friendship, and work. Despite these similarities, there are also important differences. Jews are less likely to place a high value on religion and are more likely to place great importance on a variety of civil liberties issues, including freedom of the press, freedom of speech, and the separation of church and state, especially as it is embodied in the banning of school prayer.

NOTE

1. See Appendix A for fuller discussion of sampling methodology.

11

THE PERCEPTION AND EXPERIENCE OF ANTI-SEMITIC INCIDENTS

While the level of anti-Semitic beliefs in the United States has declined since 1964, there has been ample evidence of the continued existence of anti-Semitism as a serious social problem. In 1981, the Anti-Defamation League of B'nai B'rith reported 974 anti-Semitic episodes in the United States, up sharply over 1980. While the rise may be, in part, due to different reporting procedures and other methodological factors, the overall conclusions of the 1980 ADL audit stand.

> Anti-Jewish episodes of the kind reported here substantiate what studies have shown over the years—that a disturbingly high quotient of anti-Semitism and anti-Jewish hostility exists just beneath the surface of American life. The overt, if largely unorganized and random, anti-Semitic activity apparent in the reported 1980 episodes is further visible evidence of this widespread anti-Jewish hostility—the tip of a sociological iceberg of anti-Jewish attitudes.
>
> With the exception of one case, there is little evidence that the reported episodes resulted from organized activity by anti-Jewish groups. Rather, they appear to be the work of hostile individuals acting without organizational direction.
>
> The findings underscore once again that anti-Semitism remains a virulent social disease. What is called for is greater public concern, manifested through strengthened law enforcement, realistic penalties, and expanded educational programs.[1]

The current study had its origin in a deep concern about a possible rise in anti-Semitism in the United States. This concern was prompted by a rash of anti-Semitic incidents in the United States and around the world that followed the bombing of the rue Copernic synagogue in Paris. Interestingly enough, the 1964 study[2] that forms the baseline for the present effort was prompted by remarkably similar events. On Christmas Day, 1959, a Cologne synagogue was desecrated. By the following March, at least 643 similar incidents had occurred in the United States alone.[3] As a result of this outbreak, the Anti-Defamation League of B'nai B'rith decided to launch a research program—the University of California's five-year study of anti-Semitism in the United States,[4] one of the projects of which was Selznick and Steinberg's work, *The Tenacity of Prejudice.*

EXPOSURE TO ANTI-SEMITIC INCIDENTS

The current survey provides strong support for the Anti-Defamation League's contention that reports of anti-Semitic incidents represent the "tip of a sociological iceberg." Both Jews and non-Jews were asked whether they had seen a variety of types of anti-Semitic incidents where they live or work during the previous year or two. The survey results indicate that four out of ten (39 percent) non-Jews and eight out of ten (79 percent) Jews have been exposed to anti-Semitic incidents where they live or work. Among non-Jews with Jews in their neighborhood, the figure is one out of two (47 percent). Clearly, we are talking, then, about thousands of incidents at a minimum.

The gravity of the anti-Semitic incidents that have been observed varies widely. The most common form that they take is anti-Jewish remarks at work or in the media, a form that might be relatively innocuous. However, a significant proportion of Jews say that they have had recent experience (in the last year or two) with such serious anti-Semitic incidents as the desecration of a temple (26 percent), a worker being passed over for a promotion because he or she is Jewish (10 percent), or a club that excludes Jews from membership (14 percent).

The awareness of anti-Semitic incidents among non-Jews does not appear to be significantly tied to their own level of prejudice; 40 percent of the prejudiced individuals and 44 percent of the unprejudiced are aware of anti-Semitic incidents in their area during the previous year or two. One issue raised by reports of the number of incidents in the nation, such as those reported by the ADL, is their impact on anti-Semitic beliefs. Here there are at least two distinct points of view. On the one hand, one could argue that reports of rising levels of anti-Semitic incidents might serve to reinforce the beliefs of the prejudiced minority. That is, these reports might lead the minority of Americans who are prejudiced to believe their out-

Table 11.1. Awareness of Anti-Semitic Incidents in Own Area among All Respondents

	Total (%)	Non-Jews Total (%)	with Jews in neighborhood (%)	Jews (%)
Have you seen any of the following kinds of incidents in your neighborhood or where you work in the last year or two?	40	39	47	79
Anti-Jewish remarks where you live or work	13	13	19	40
Anti-Jewish remarks on TV, radio, newspapers	11	11	14	31
Anti-Jewish graffiti on buildings or vehicles	7	6	9	36
Social clubs/groups that restrict Jewish membership	6	5	7	14
Desecration of temples	3	3	4	26
Worker passed over for a promotion because he/she is Jewish	2	2	2	10
None	60	61	53	21

look is more widespread and therefore more acceptable. On the other hand, one could argue that such reports could serve to rally those who are unprejudiced or neutral to a more active support for more tolerant attitudes. The question is far from answered, and the study of the impact of such reports is an important issue for future research on anti-Semitism.

PERCEIVED TRENDS IN ANTI-SEMITISM

It is surprising that Jews are consistently more likely than non-Jews to be aware of anti-Semitic incidents in their neighborhood or workplace. This greater awareness could be expected as the natural outgrowth of the greater salience of anti-Semitic behavior for Jews. Consistent with the sharp contrast in the perceptions of Jews and non-Jews regarding current levels of anti-Semitism is the contrast in beliefs about the trend in anti-Semitism. Most non-Jews who are aware of anti-Semitic incidents believe that they are stable or declining in number. Many (42 percent) Jews who are aware of anti-Semitic incidents, on the other hand, believe that the number has risen in recent years.

The question of salience is, of course, critical here as well. In the months preceding this survey, many print and broadcast media reported stories about the rising number of anti-Semitic incidents. The most common source of these stories was statistics gathered by the Anti-Defamation League. Jews were, no doubt, more likely than non-Jews to have followed these stories closely.

In addition to believing that the number of anti-Semitic incidents is rising, most (67 percent) Jews believe that an increase in anti-Semitism in the United States is possible and 40 percent believe an increase in anti-Semitism in their own area is possible. These views of Jews conflicts sharply, again, with the views of non-Jews—few of whom believe a rise in anti-Semitism is possible in their area (7 percent) or elsewhere in the country (21 percent).

Table 11.2. Perceived Frequency of Anti-Semitic Incidents among All Who Were Aware of Any

	Total (%)	Non-Jews (%)	Jews (%)
Compared to five to ten years ago			
More anti-Semitic incidents	23	22	44
Same number of anti-Semitic incidents	38	38	34
Fewer anti-Semitic incidents	37	38	22
Not sure	2	2	0
Net difference:			
More-less	-14	-16	+22

The history of anti-Semitism is long and bitter. Many times in the past, the position of Jews had been well established only to unravel as the result of the irrationality of anti-Semitic prejudice. Given this long history, it should come as no surprise that American Jews are more preoccupied with the possibility of anti-Semitism than are non-Jews.

JEWS' PERCEPTIONS ABOUT HOW OTHER AMERICANS REGARD THEM

The disparity between the beliefs of Jews and non-Jews about the extent and trend in anti-Semitic incidents exists as well in the area of anti-Semitic beliefs. The perceptions of Jews about their position in the United States appear to be sharply at odds with the views expressed by non-Jews. Jewish perceptions are consistently more negative than the views actually expressed by non-Jews. For example, most (76 percent) Jews feel that the majority of non-Jews believe "Jews have too much power in the business world." Among non-

Table 11.3. Beliefs about Jews versus Jewish Perception of Those Beliefs

	Non-Jews (%)	Jews' perceptions of the views held by the majority of non-Jews (%)
Jews have more money than most people.	56	83
Jews are more ambitious than other people.	45	79
Jews have too much power in the business world.	32	76
Jews have too much power in the United States.	20	53
Jews try to push in where they are not wanted.	16	55
I am bothered by the feeling that Jews have more money than most people.[a]	13	77

[a]Based on those who hold the belief.
Note: These are questions 8b, 8a, 10b, 10a, 9 and 8c, Appendix D.

Jews, one in three (32 percent) actually express this belief. Similarly, the majority (55 percent) of Jews feel that non-Jews see them as trying to "push in where they are not wanted." In contrast, only one in six (16 percent) non-Jews express this belief.

Jones provides us with an explanation of the differences in perception between Jews and non-Jews in their analysis of the difference in the views of actors and observers.

> Actors tend to attribute the causes of their behavior to stimuli inherent in the situation, while observers tend to attribute behavior to stable disproportions of the actor. This is due in part to the actor's more detailed knowledge of his circumstances, history, motives and experiences. Perhaps more importantly, the tendency is a result of the differential salience of the information available to the actor and observer. . . . Behavior is thus seen by the observer to be a manifestation of the actor and seen by the actor to be a response to the situation.[5]

According to the Jones thesis, Jews could be expected to err in over-attributing anti-Semitic sentiments to non-Jews, whose "negative" actions were in fact a response to their perceived situation rather than to stable dispositions (anti-Semitism).

Another area where a sizeable disparity exists between Jewish perceptions and the expressed beliefs of non-Jews is that of social acceptance. The social acceptance of Jews as potential marriage partners, neighbors, and political candidates is relatively high. Generally speaking, the social acceptability of Jews is equal to that of Italian Americans and significantly greater than that of Japanese Americans and Black Americans. In contrast to this relatively high level of acceptability expressed by non-Jews, Jewish respondents, by and large, believe that Jews are seen as unacceptable as presidential candidates or as marriage partners.

The differences in outlook of Jews and non-Jews was also reflected in public reaction to the preliminary reports of the findings of the current study. When released to the press in the summer of 1981 they were widely reported in a matter-of-fact way by most of the major media. However the reaction of the Anglo-Jewish press was often quite different. The following quotation from a news commentary is representative of a number of Anglo-Jewish newspapers.

> The statistics further substantiate that anti-Semitism is a fact of life in this country which affects the very structure of democracy. In past

Table 11.4. Social Distance: Jewish Perceptions versus
Beliefs of Non-Jews

	Non-Jews (%)	Jews' perceptions of the views held by the majority of non-Jews (%)
Would be bothered very much/somewhat if my political party nominated a Jew for president	21	78
Would object strongly/somewhat if own child wanted to marry a Jew	28	62
Would prefer not to have any Jews in neighborhood	6	20

years we have witnessed a rise in overt anti-Semitic acts including desecration of synagogues and cemeteries, a continual buildup of hate literature throughout this country and worldwide, but which originates here
in the U.S., parades and support for neo-Nazis and the Ku-Klux-Klan,
and the continued pursuit by historical revisionists who claim the Holocaust a hoax and that genocide was not a policy of the Nazi regime.

The report presents illusions by suggesting a decrease in anti-
Semitism by implying that because a generation has passed on since the
last survey, it has been replaced by a younger, less anti-Semitic one
resulting in a subsequent decrease in anti-Semitism. American Jewry
should know all too well that numbers are deceptive and in this time of
social disarray and economic instability, the fuel is there for those who
seek scapegoats. As the Jewish community knows best, Jews are an
easy target.[6]

JEWISH IDENTITY

While Jews' perceptions often conflict with the expressed beliefs
of non-Jews, one area where there is considerable agreement is on the
question of Jewish identity. A substantial majority of Jews and a
majority of non-Jews with an opinion believe that Jews are losing
their distinctive identity. However, though many Jews and non-Jews
share similar perceptions, their evaluations are quite different. Most

non-Jews regard the loss of Jewish identity as a good trend, while the majority of Jews believe that it is not a good trend. Interestingly, the belief that Jews are losing their identity is significantly more widespread among those non-Jews who are least prejudiced, indicating that their greater acceptance of Jews is, in part, tied to their belief that Jews are assimilating into the larger culture. This assimilationist perspective is, of course, quite different from one that truly tolerates cultural differences.

Table 11.5. Views of the Distinctive Identity of Jews among All Respondents

	Non-Jews (%)	Jews (%)
Are Jews losing their distinctive identity?		
Yes	41	69
No	36	21
Not sure	23	10
Is this loss of identity[a]		
A good trend	74	28
Not a good trend	9	59
Not sure	17	13

[a]Based on those who believe Jews are losing their distinctive identity.

SUMMARY

Four out of ten non-Jews and the vast majority (79 percent) of Jews have been exposed to anti-Semitic incidents in the last year or two where they live or work. These incidents ranged from anti-Jewish remarks in the media to the desecration of temples. Generally speaking, non-Jews tend to see these incidents as declining in frequency or remaining the same, while Jews tend to see them as increasing in frequency.

As might be expected, there is a sharp contrast between Jews and non-Jews when it comes to the experiences and perception of anti-Semitic incidents. Jews are more likely to be aware of them, believe they are on the rise, and think a resurgency of anti-Semitism is possible.

Jewish perceptions about the position of Jews in America appear to be sharply at odds with the views actually expressed by non-Jews in that they are consistently more negative. For example:

Most Jews (76 percent) feel that the majority of non-Jews believe "Jews have too much power in the business world." Among non-Jews, one out of three (32 percent) actually express this belief.

A majority (55 percent) of Jews feel that the majority of non-Jews believe Jews are trying to "push in where they are not wanted." In fact, only one in six (16 percent) non-Jews express this belief. Also, the perceived "pushiness" of Jews is substantially less than the perceived "pushiness" of Black Americans and no greater than that of Italian Americans.

In contrast to the relatively high level of acceptance of Jews expressed by non-Jews, the majority of Jewish respondents believe that Jews are seen as unacceptable as marriage partners or as presidential candidates.

NOTES

1. "1981 Audit of Anti-Semitic Incidents" (New York: Anti-Defamation League of B'nai B'rith), mimeographed, p. 4.

2. G. Selznick and S. Steinberg, *The Tenacity of Prejudice* (New York: Harper & Row, 1969).

3. See D. Caplovitz and C. Rogers, *Swastika 1960: The Epidemic of Anti-Semitic Vandalism in America* (New York: Anti Defamation League of B'nai B'rith, 1960).

4. See Chapter 2, note 2 for the key studies of that research effort.

5. E. E. Jones, et al., "The Actor and the Observer" in *Attribution: Perceiving The Causes of Behavior* (Morristown, N.J.: General Learning Press, 1972), p. 93.

6. B. Smolar, "Between You and Me," (Los Angeles: *B'nai B'rith Messenger*, August 28, 1981), p. 25.

12

CONCLUSION

This final chapter is a summary of the major conclusions of the study and their implications for the future of attitudes toward Jews in the United States.

ANTI-SEMITISM IN THE UNITED STATES:
WIDESPREAD BUT DECLINING

In the absence of any historical trend or comparison group against which anti-Jewish sentiments could be gauged, the level of anti-Semitic beliefs uncovered in the current study would be alarming. Nearly one in four (23 percent) Americans can be characterized as anti-Semitic and only one out of two (45 percent) are relatively free of prejudice. Those who are characterized as anti-Semitic are far from mild in their negative judgement about Jews.[1] A majority of those who are prejudiced accept virtually every negative stereotype.

The level of anti-Semitism in the United States clearly remains a serious social problem. However, while anti-Semitism continues to be quite pervasive, the results of the current study provide encouragement about recent trends and reason for cautious optimism about the future. First, the results of the study indicate that many anti-Semitic beliefs have become less widespread since 1964. This is particularly true when it comes to traditional negative stereotypes about Jewish character (for example, shrewdness and irritating faults). It must be pointed out that the decline in anti-Semitic beliefs has not been universal. There has been increased concern about Jewish power and loyalty to Israel. However, on balance, the overall trend is in the direction of less prejudice.

Second, it is clear that prejudice against Jews relative to other ethnic and racial groups is not particularly pervasive. As might be expected, the level of acceptance of Jewish Americans is much greater than that of Black Americans or Japanese Americans. The comparison with Italian Americans is perhaps more interesting. Jews and Italian Americans are equally likely to be accepted as neighbors, political candidates, and potential spouses for one's own children. In terms of attitudes, even in the critical area of the perception of power, Jews and Italian Americans are viewed quite similarly. Approximately one in five Americans view either Jews or Italian Americans as having "too much power." Indeed, the only area where Jews are more likely to be viewed negatively than Italian, Japanese, or Black Americans is in the related areas of money and business power.

THE DYNAMICS OF PREJUDICE

Selznick and Steinberg concluded their 1964 analysis with the observation that "anti-Semitism continues at significant levels, and lack of education is the primary factor in its acceptance."[2] This observation continues to hold today. A low level of education appears to continue as the mainspring that drives anti-Semitism. The effects of education are not completely independent; they are closely intertwined with other demographic factors, notably age and race. Also, the effects of all of these demographic factors are mediated by a number of nondemographic factors. The overall model of anti-Semitism that emerges in the current study is represented in Figure 12.1.

The model concisely summarizes the major dynamics of anti-Semitic prejudice as they are described in the current study. Education, age, and race all have significant effects. Prejudice is more widespread among those who are older, less educated, and black. In addition to these direct effects, the background factors are associated with three other variables that have strong associations with anti-Semitism. Prejudice against Jews is less widespread among those who are low in xenophobia, are favorable in their views of Israel, and have higher levels of contact with Jews.

Figure 12.1. The Dynamics of Prejudice

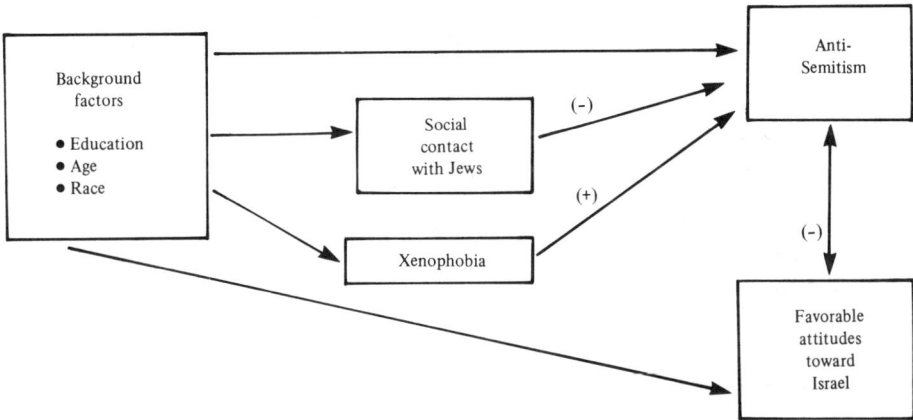

Table 12.1 presents the zero order and partial correlations of the major variables used in the analysis and provides a brief summary of the major findings of the study. These are:

Age, education, and race are all important factors in explaining the level of anti-Semitism in the United States. Each has a unique effect though there is also considerable overlap in their effects. Together these three demographic factors explain 11 percent of the variance in anti-Semitism.

Five significant nondemographic factors stand out in explaining anti-Semitism, including xenophobia, attitudes toward Israel, religiousness and religious fundamentalism, and social contact with Jews. After controlling for age, education, and race, we find that only two factors stand out as significant—xenophobia and attitudes toward Israel—indicating that the effects of religion and social contrast are almost entirely due to the three background factors (age, education, and race).

Table 12.1. Zero Order and Partial Correlations with
Anti-Semitism Index

	Zero order correlation with anti-Semitism	Partial correlation controlling for		
		Education	Race	Age
Demographic factors				
Education	-.25	—	—	—
Race (white/black)	.21	.19	—	—
Age	.17	.12	.13	—
Variance explained by education, race, and age (R²)	11%			
Nondemographic factors				
Xenophobia	.37	.30	.31	.29
Attitude toward Israel	.22	-.19	-.18	-.19
Social contact with Jews	-.13	-.05	-.04	-.04
Religiousness	.11	.07	.06	.04
Religion fundamentalist	.10	.06	.02	.01
Variation explained by all eight variables (R²)	23%			

DECLINING ANTI-SEMITISM: GENERATIONAL CHANGE, NOT MATURATION

One of the most critical findings of the study is the observation that the decline in the level of anti-Semitic belief has come about primarily because of generational change. That is, it has resulted from the fact that, as time has passed, a younger, better-educated, and more tolerant generation has replaced an older, more intolerant one.

This finding has a number of significant implications. It suggests that an individual's attitudes toward Jews are probably relatively enduring. While this cannot be confirmed without panel data, it appears quite probable that the stability of the cohort means between 1964 and 1981 is due to the stability of individual attitudes. It also suggests that the decline in anti-Semitism should continue as the better-educated and more tolerant young adults continue through the life cycle, ultimately replacing today's current crop of older adults. Particularly encouraging in this respect is the fact that today's young adults are even less prejudiced than were those in the mid-1960s.

FACTORS NOT ASSOCIATED WITH ANTI-SEMITISM

Perhaps almost as encouraging as the decline in anti-Semitic beliefs is the variety of factors that the current study indicates are not related to anti-Semitism.

Political Attitudes

There are many indications in the current study that anti-Semitic beliefs are not tied to political beliefs. For example, anti-Semitic attitudes are not significantly associated with a respondent's self-described political outlook, how he or she voted in the 1980 presidential election, or whether he or she has grown more conservative or more liberal in recent years. There is no evidence, then, that anti-Semitism is tied to political ideology among the vast majority of Americans. This does not mean that there may not be tiny groups of politically minded anti-Semites. It simply means that for the masses, politics and anti-Semitism appear to bear very little relationship to one another.

Religious Affiliation and Religious Belief

Religious affiliation and religious belief, on the other hand, are related to anti-Semitism. The level of anti-Semitism is higher among individuals with highly traditional religious beliefs and those who belong to more conservative denominations. However, what is critical here is that the apparent effects of religion are due to the fact that traditional religious affiliation and belief are more common among individuals who are older, less educated, and nonwhite—all groups that are more likely to be composed of anti-Semites. It is the effect of these background factors and not religion that contributes to the apparent connection between traditional Christian beliefs and anti-Semitism.

Economic Issues

One commonly expressed fear in the Jewish community over the past few years is that Jews may become the scapegoat for the nation's general economic condition or, more specifically, for the rise of oil prices and the turmoil in the Middle East. The current study finds no evidence of a connection between anti-Semitism and concern about recession, unemployment, an energy shortage, or a war in the Middle East.

The absence of any relationship between anti-Semitism and these domestic and international concerns is consistent with the decline in anti-Semitism in recent years.

BLACK-JEWISH RELATIONS

The current study leaves little doubt that there is widespread prejudice against Jews in the black community. Only one in five (22 percent) blacks can be characterized as unprejudiced, compared to nearly one out of two (47 percent) whites. However, there is also evidence that black anti-Jewish sentiment is to a considerable extent actually the reflection of more general anti-white sentiment. Indeed, the social acceptance of Jews by blacks is essentially the same as black social acceptance of Italian Americans.

To the extent that black prejudice against Jews is uniquely directed at Jews, it appears to stem from economic sources. One factor that appears to contribute to negative feelings toward Jews among blacks is the social interaction between the two groups, which tends to be economic and impersonal.

ISRAEL AND AMERICAN JEWS

Regardless of their background or political views, Americans continue to be strong supporters of the State of Israel. Indeed, this widespread support exists even among those non-Jews who are prejudiced in their outlook toward Jews.

Despite the strength of this support, when this survey was conducted in the late winter of 1981, there were many indications that it was eroding because of a growing sentiment among Americans that the Israelis should negotiate with the PLO to bring a settlement to the Palestinian issue. And the increased number of incidents in West Bank towns since 1981 has probably increased American impatience for a negotiated settlement.

Nevertheless, the high regard in which Israel is held indicates that the position of Jews in the United States has not been hurt by the State of Israel. If it has had any effect on Americans' attitudes toward Jews, it is likely that it has been favorable.

THE FUTURE OF TOLERANCE IN THE UNITED STATES

The past two decades have been a time of turmoil and tension in U.S. society. An all too familiar litany of events has shocked the nation—political assassinations, race riots, the Vietnam War, Watergate, Abscam, the energy crisis, the Iranian crisis, inflation, recession, and more. However, despite all of this turmoil, the nation has grown increasingly tolerant of diversity.

This fact, together with the increasing levels of education, leads us to believe that, should this trend study be replicated again in another 17 years, researchers will find the United States entering the year 2000 as a still more tolerant nation.

NOTES

1. See Table 4.1.
2. G. Selznick and S. Steinberg, *The Tenacity of Prejudice* (New York: Harper & Row, 1969), p. 184.

APPENDIX A:
SAMPLE DESCRIPTION

This study's sample was designed to accomplish several objectives: represent the population of the contiguous United States ages 18 years and older; maximize the efficiency and accuracy of the sample by utilizing a series of innovative but proven sampling techniques; utilize the latest population data available; adequately represent the Jewish and Black population of the United States while maintaining the integrity of the national sample data reported.

These objectives were accomplished through the use of two independent but integrated samples: 1. the General Public sample, comprising 1,072 interviews, was designed to be representative of the population ages 18 years and older; 2. the Jewish/Black (supplemental) sample, comprising 143 interviews, was designed to be representative of these groups. The two samples were integrated by statistical weighting so that the data reported are representative of the population of the contiguous United States ages 18 years and older with the Jewish/Black segment of that population being representative of that supplemental group in the contiguous United States.

THE GENERAL PUBLIC SAMPLE

The data used in implementing this sample were total final population statistics for states and Standard Metropolitan Statistical Areas as compiled in the 1970 Census of the United States, and updated by Yankelovich, Skelly and White, Inc. to reflect the population as of December 31, 1974. These data reported on the population of: each of the states and the District of Columbia; the counties within the states (and county subdivisions in New England); all incorporated places with 1,000 or more population; the Standard Metropolitan Statistical Areas (SMSA); the central city and noncentral city population distribution within each SMSA; the counties (or portions of counties in New England) falling within each SMSA.

CHOOSING CLUSTER POINTS

The total population of the United States was stratified by the nine standard Census Divisions: New England; Middle Atlantic; East

North Central; West North Central; South Atlantic; East South Central; West South Central; Mountain; West; and within the nine divisions by Metropolitan (SMSA) and non-Metropolitan Area. The nine Metropolitan Area strata were then ordered by size of population, specific SMSA's were ordered by size of population within each divisional stratum, and counties (or county subdivisions) were ordered by size of population within each SMSA.

Having ordered the population in this manner, 135 primary sampling units were obtained. Selection from the arrays was on the basis of fixed intervals with random starting points. The interval used for the selection of non-Metropolitan clusters reflected the fact that these clusters would be represented at one-half their normal weight. A weighting procedure was utilized to bring these clusters back to their true representation.

CHOOSING STARTING POINTS IN THE SUPPLEMENTAL SAMPLES

The cluster points for the Jewish/Black supplemental samples were based on extending those clusters of the general sample that had yielded two or more interviews with members of the respective groups.

RESPONDENT SELECTION IN THE SUPPLEMENTAL SAMPLES

As in the general sample, interviewers in the supplemental samples followed a set of detailed and specific standard instructions for proceeding through the assigned cluster from that starting point. These route-selection procedures were described in great detail in the sampling instructions. Respondent selection in households along the route followed a number of specific procedures designed to minimize the effect of sex-skewed sample execution. In order to determine eligibility for the Jewish sample, potential respondents were screened on a number of questions including items bearing on the observation of religious holidays. Within each eligible household, the eligible respondent (18 years of age or older) was selected by a random selection process. Once a respondent was designated, there was no substitution of this eligible household member. Only *one* interview per household was completed.

APPENDIX B:
CORRELATION MATRIX OF
ITEMS IN ANTI-SEMITISM INDEX

Beliefs in index	A	B	C	D	E	F	G	H	I	J
a. Too much power in U.S.	–	–	–	–	–	–	–	–	–	–
b. Care only about own kind	.297	–	–	–	–	–	–	–	–	–
c. Not as honest as other businessmen	-.183	-.262	–	–	–	–	–	–	–	–
d. Too much power in business world	.530	.287	-.227	–	–	–	–	–	–	–
e. More loyal to Israel than to America	.220	.324	-.174	.207	–	–	–	–	–	–
f. Control international banking	.285	.263	-.123	.242	.273	–	–	–	–	–
g. Shrewd and tricky in business	.246	.429	-.273	.211	.265	.323	–	–	–	–
h. Have a lot of irritating faults	.182	.326	-.210	.173	.273	.240	.323	–	–	–
i. Use shady practices to get ahead	.242	.383	-.365	.265	.302	.250	.481	.390	–	–
j. Stick together too much	.206	.302	-.169	.272	.251	.273	.309	.295	.269	–
k. Always like to head things	.231	.329	-.157	.290	.261	.318	.301	.303	.319	.324

Average inter-item correlation = .275; short form alpha = .81.

APPENDIX C:
FACTOR ANALYSIS OF KEY INDEXES

The following are the items and the rotated principal component factor scores for the indexes used in the current study. Each content area was factor analyzed separately.

1. ANTI-SEMITISM INDEX

Twenty-two items measuring attitudes toward Jews were factor analyzed. The following four factor solution replicates to a remarkable degree the factor structure obtained in 1964. Because of the stability of the factor structure and to maintain comparability with the early study the 11-item index was used again in the current analysis. The reliability coefficient for the 11-item index was .79.

The following items have been assigned to Factor 1:

*Jewish employers go out of their way to hire other Jews.	.624
*Jewish businessmen are so shrewd and tricky; other people don't have a fair chance in competition.	.606
Jews are stubborn and resist change.	.592
*Jews don't care what happens to anyone but their own kind.	.576
*Jews are more willing than others to use shady practices to get what they want.	.576
*Jews have a lot of irritating faults.	.562
*Jews always like to be at the head of things.	.557
*Jews are more loyal to Israel than to the United States.	.544
*Jews stick together too much.	.541
Jews are always stirring up trouble with their ideas.	.488
Jews should stop complaining about what happened to them in Nazi Germany.	.441

The following items have been assigned to Factor 2:

Jews are warm and friendly people.	.648

---

*Items in anti-Semitism index.

Jews have contributed much to the cultural life of the
    United States.   .594
Jews have a strong faith in God.   .584
Jews are usually hard working people.   .548
*Jews are just as honest as other businessmen.   .503

The following variables have been assigned to Factor 3:

*Do you think that Jews have too much power in the
    United States?   .764
*In the business world Jews have too much power.   .741
  Are Jews trying to push in where they are not wanted?   .603

The following variables have been assigned to Factor 4:

Level of ambition of Jews   .762
Amount of money that Jews have   .749
Are Jews family oriented or not?   .404

2. XENOPHOBIA INDEX

Item	Factor loading
It bothers me to see immigrants succeeding more than Americans who were born here.	.643

    Agree   = 1
    Disagree   = 3
    Not sure/no answer = 2

Nothing in other countries can beat the American way
of life.   .519

    Agree   = 1
    Disagree   = 3
    Not sure/no answer = 2

---

*Items in anti-Semitism index.

Foreigners who come to live in the United States should
give up their foreign ways and learn to be like other
Americans.   .655

  Agree   = 1
  Disagree   = 3
  Not sure/no answer   = 2

The illegal alien situation is one of the most serious
problems in the United States.   .617

  Agree   = 1
  Disagree   = 3
  Not sure/no answer   = 2

Scoring Index	Percent Distribution
High level of xenophobia is a score of 4–6.	35%
Medium level of xenophobia is a score of 7–9.	36%
Low level of xenophobia is a score of 10–12.	29%

3. RELIGIOUS CONVICTION INDEX

Item	Factor loading
Please look at this card and tell me which statement comes closest to expressing what you believe about God.	.736

  I don't believe in God.   = 6
  I don't know whether there is a God and I
    don't believe there is any way to find out.   = 5
  I don't believe in a personal God, but I do
    believe in a higher power of some kind.   = 4
  I find myself believing in God some of the
    time, but not at other times.   = 3

Item	Factor loading
While I have doubts, I feel that I do believe in God. = 2	
I know God really exists and I have no doubts about it. = 1	
Not sure/no answer. = 3	

How sure are you that there is a life beyond death?
Are you absolutely sure or pretty sure that there is
a life beyond death or are you absolutely or pretty
sure that there is *no* life beyond death?   .740

    Absolutely sure there is a life beyond death = 1
    Pretty sure there is a life beyond death = 2
    Absolutely sure there is no life beyond death = 3
    Pretty sure there is no life beyond death = 4
    Not sure/no answer = 2

All in all, how important would you say religion is
to you—extremely important, quite important, fairly
important, not too important, or not important at
all?   .70

    Extremely important = 1
    Quite important = 2
    Fairly important = 3
    Not too important = 4
    Not important at all = 5
    Not sure/no answer = 3

Scoring of Index	Percent distribution
High level of religious conviction is a score of 3–4.	42%
Medium level of religious conviction is a score of 5–6.	27%
Low level of religious conviction is a score of 7–15.	31%

4. CHRISTIAN FUNDAMENTALISM

Item	Factor loadings
We've heard a lot in the last few years about individuals who have been "born again." Have you personally had such an experience?	.801

Yes	= 1
No	= 3
Not sure	= 2
No answer	= 2

Item	Factor loadings
Do you think that a person who doesn't accept Jesus can be saved?	.753

Yes	= 3
No	= 1
Other	= 2
Not sure/no answer	= 2

Item	Factor loadings
What about the belief that the Devil actually exists? Are you absolutely sure or are you pretty sure that the Devil exists or are you absolutely sure or pretty sure that the Devil does not exist?	.604

Absolutely sure there is a devil.	= 1
Pretty sure there is a devil.	= 1
Absolutely sure there is no devil.	= 3
Pretty sure there is no devil.	= 3
Not sure/no answer.	= 2

Scoring of index	Percent distribution
High level of Christian fundamentalism is a score of 3–5.	39%
Low level of Christian fundamentalism is a score of 6–7.	35%
Nonfundamentalists are those with a score of 8–9.	26%

5. ATTITUDES TOWARD ISRAEL INDEX

Item	Factor loadings
Let me ask a few questions about Israel. First of all, do you think that it is very important that we continue to support Israel, somewhat important, or not important at all?	.809

    Very important   = 1
    Somewhat important = 2
    Not important at all = 3
    Not sure/no answer = 2

Item	Factor loadings
Do you feel that the continuation of Israel as a Jewish state is important or not important to our country and people like yourself?	.729

    Important   = 1
    Not important   = 2
    Not sure/no answer = 2

Item	Factor loadings
In view of the situation in the Middle East, do you feel that the United States should increase its present military aid to Israel, continue it at the same level as now, or cut it back?	.661

    Increase   = 1
    Same   = 2
    Cut it back   = 3
    Not sure/no answer = 2

Item	Factor loadings
Suppose there were a war between the Arab nations and Israel. Which side do you think *you* would personally sympathize with?	.629

    Arab nations   = 3
    Israel   = 1

Neither   = 2
Not sure/no answer = 2

Scoring of index	Percent distribution
Highly favorable attitudes is a score of 4–6.	32%
Moderately favorable attitudes is a score of 7–8.	41%
Unfavorable attitudes is a score of 9–11.	27%

APPENDIX D:
THE QUESTIONNAIRES

YANKELOVICH, SKELLY AND WHITE, INC.

Job #8225
January, 1981

1-
2-
3-
4-
5-

AMERICAN ATTITUDES

<u>VERSION A</u>

NAME: _____ CF#: _____ ☐☐☐☐☐☐☐☐☐

ADDRESS: _____ City: _____ STATE: _____ ZIP CODE: _____

TELEPHONE #:(   ) _____ Time Started: _____ Time Ended: _____

INTERVIEWER: _____ VALIDATED: _____ DATE: _____

COMPLETE RESPONDENT'S IDENTIFICATION AT END OF INTERVIEW.

<u>NOTE:</u> The study made use of two questionnaires
<u>VERSIONS:</u> They are reproduced below in a single
combined version.

Version A - Administered to Non-Jews

Version B - Administered to Jews.

SCREENER - Supplement I

(American Attitudes Study)

Hello, I'm _____, from Yankelovich, Skelly and White, In
We're doing a study of attitudes toward a variety of political, social and economic issues, and
I'd like to ask you a few questions.

1. (IF NECESSARY) First, may I speak with someone who is 18 years of age or older?

                          (TERMINATE) - No adult (18 years or older) at home.....67-1

2. Are you or is anyone in your family employed by a marketing research firm or an
    advertising agency?

                                      (TERMINATE) - Yes.....68-1
                                                    No....... -2

3. In order to determine who should answer the next questions, I need the first names or
    initials in alphabetical order of the members of your household 18 years of age and
    older who are presently at home. Please list the males first, then the females.

                              _____

                              _____

                              _____

                              _____

                              _____

                              _____

RESPONDENT SELECTION INSTRUCTIONS

At the first household you contact, the selected respondent is the <u>first name</u> listed above.

At the second household, your respondent will be the <u>last name</u> listed above.

Continue alternating the <u>first</u> and <u>last name</u> listed above to identify the eligible respondent until you have completed your quota.

When you have completed a sex quota, ask only for the names of those persons who are of the sex needed to complete your assignment.

<u>NOTE:</u> After you have determined the selected respondent, <u>NO</u> substitutions are allowed in that household.

69 = g

80-5

4. Which of the holidays on this list are important to you now or were when you were a child? Just call off the numbers from the Screener Card.

CARD 6

1.	July 4th, Independence Day....	5-1
2.	Christmas.................	6-1
3.	Labor Day.................	7-1
4.	Chanukah..................	8-1
5.	Martin Luther King Day......	9-1
6.	Columbus Day..............	10-1
7.	St. Patrick's Day..........	11-1
8.	Passover..................	12-1
9.	Memorial Day..............	13-1
10.	Easter...................	14-1
11.	Yom Kippur................	15-1
12.	Thanksgiving..............	16-1
13.	Good Friday...............	17-1
14.	Rosh Hashana..............	18-1
15.	Flag Day..................	19-1
16.	Palm Sunday...............	20-1

5. Some people consider themselves Italian Americans, others Polish Americans, Black Americans, Jewish Americans, and so on. What group, if any, do you identify with? (RECORD VERBATIM AND CIRCLE BELOW)

(Record verbatim and circle below)

German/Austrian American	21-1
Irish American	22-1
Black American	23-1
Italian American	24-1
Polish American	25-1
Spanish American	26-1
Scandinavian American	27-1
French American	28-1
Scottish American	29-1
American Indian	30-1
Jewish	31-1
Chinese	32-1
Japanese	33-1
Other	34-1
None/Just American	35-1
	36-1
	37-1

IF RESPONDENT MENTIONS JEWISH, RESPONDENT QUALIFIES FOR JEWISH SUPPLEMENTAL ASSIGNMENT. (USE VERSION 'B' OF QUESTIONNAIRE.)

ALL OTHERS...TERMINATE.

CF#: 38-39-40-41-42- 43-44-45- 46-47-48-

Respondent's Name: _____

Interviewer: _____

Date: _____

PLEASE ATTACH SCREENER TO BACK OF COMPLETED QUESTIONNAIRE

136

Version

A & B

We're interested in finding out how people all over the country feel about some important issues of the day, including how they feel about certain groups.

1a. First of all, how do you feel things are going in the country these days — very well, fairly well, pretty badly or very badly?

Very well.......... 6-1
Fairly well........ -2
Pretty badly....... -3
Very badly......... -4

A & B

1b. In commenting on how things are going in the country, some people tell us that the problems are no worse than at any other time in recent years. Others say that the country is in deep and serious trouble. Which comes closest to your own feelings — the fact that: (READ LIST AND RECORD ONE ANSWER)

Problems are no worse than at other times...... 7-1
The country is in deep and serious trouble...... -2
Not sure (VOLUNTEERED)............ -3

A & B

1c. Do you have a lot of confidence, some confidence, or no real confidence that in a few years from now, our country will be strong and prosperous?

A lot of confidence...... 8-1
Some confidence.......... -2
No real confidence....... -3

A & B

1d. People all have different concerns. Will you tell me for each of the following statements whether right now this is something that worries you personally a lot, a little or not at all at the present time? (READ LIST AND RECORD ONE ANSWER FOR EACH STATEMENT)

	A Lot	A Little	Not At All
Losing your job because of the economy....	9 -1	-2	-3
A recession in the country...............	10-1	-2	-3
An energy shortage in the country........	11-1	-2	-3
Another war in the Middle East...........	12-1	-2	-3
The possibility of a world war...........	13-1	-2	-3

A & B 2a. Do you feel the United States is losing power in the world or is it becoming more powerful?

Losing power............................ 14-1
Becoming more powerful.................. -2
Staying the same (VOLUNTEERED)......... -3
Don't know (VOLUNTEERED)............... -4

(SKIP TO Q.3)

A & B 2b. IF LOSING POWER IN Q.2a, ASK: How much does this disturb you — a great deal, somewhat, or very little?

A great deal............................ 15-1
Somewhat................................ -2
Very little............................. -3
Don't know (VOLUNTEERED)............... -4

A & B 3a. I'm going to read a list of statements to you and I would like to know whether you agree or disagree with each one. (READ STATEMENT, RECORD ONE ANSWER AND CONTINUE WITH LIST)

	Agree	Disagree	Not Sure
A. America owes a great deal to the immigrants who came here..............................	16-1	-2	-3
B. Persons who insist on wearing beards should not be allowed to teach in public schools...........	17-1	-2	-3
C. Foreigners who come to live in America should give up their foreign ways and learn to be like other Americans........................	18-1	-2	-3
D. Nothing in other countries can beat the American way of life.............................	19-1	-2	-3
E. It bothers me to see immigrants succeeding more than Americans who were born here............	20-1	-2	-3

138

F. Homosexuals should be allowed to hold office and
   teach school just like anyone else............. 21-1   -2   -3

G. The illegal alien situation is one of the most
   serious problems in the United States............ 22-1   -2   -3

A & B   3b. On the whole, do you feel that minority groups in this country are receiving too much
             attention, too little attention or just about the right amount of attention these days?

                                                        Too much attention........ 23-1
                                                        Too little attention........   -2
                                                        Right amount................   -3

A & B   4a. Suppose Congress wanted to pass a law saying that groups who disagree with our form
             of government could not hold public meetings or make speeches. As far as you know,
             would Congress have the right under the Constitution to pass such a law?

                                                        Yes................. 24-1
                                                        No..................   -2
                                                        Don't know..........   -3
                                                        (SKIP TO Q.4c)

A & B   4b. IF YES IN Q.4a, ASK: Would you be in favor of a law saying that groups who disagree
             with our form of government could not hold public meetings or make speeches, or would
             you be opposed to it?

                                                        In favor........ 25-1
                                                        Oppose............   -2
                                                        Don't know......   -3
                                                        (SKIP TO Q.5a)

A & B   4c. IF NO OR DON'T KNOW IN Q.4a, ASK: Supposing it were constitutional, would you like
             to see such a law passed or not?

                                                        Yes................. 26-1
                                                        No..................   -2
                                                        Don't know..........   -3

A & B   5a. How would you feel about a law saying that the President must be a person who believes
             in God? As far as you know, would Congress have the right under the Constitution to
             pass such a law?

                                                        Yes................. 27-1
                                                        No..................   -2
                                                        Don't know..........   -3
                                                        (SKIP TO Q.5c)

A & B 5b. IF YES IN Q.5a, ASK: Would you be in favor of a law saying that the President must be a person who believes in God, or would you be opposed to it?

In favor........ 28-1
Opposed.......... -2
Don't know....... -3

(SKIP TO Q.6)

A & B 5c. IF NO OR DON'T KNOW IN Q.5a, ASK: Supposing it were constitutional, would you like to see such a law passed or not?

Yes.............. 29-1
No............... -2
Don't know....... -3

A & B 6. (HAND CARD A) Now I'd like to know how important you personally feel each of the following are on a scale of 1 to 7, where one is very important and seven is not very important? Let's start with A, where would it fall on the scale? (RECORD ONE ANSWER AND CONTINUE WITH LIST)

	1 Very Important	2	3	4	5	6	7 Not Very Important	Not Sure
A. A strong national defense..........	30-1	-2	-3	-4	-5	-6	-7	-8
B. A federal tax cut.................	31-1	-2	-3	-4	-5	-6	-7	-8
C. Freedom of speech................	32-1	-2	-3	-4	-5	-6	-7	-8
D. Freedom of the press.............	33-1	-2	-3	-4	-5	-6	-7	-8
E. Federal job programs for the inner cities.................	34-1	-2	-3	-4	-5	-6	-7	-8

140

F. A strong U.S. economy.............	35-1	-2	-3	-4	-5	-6	-7	-8
G. Reducing air and water pollution..	36-1	-2	-3	-4	-5	-6	-7	-8
H. Providing aid for developing nations...................	37-1	-2	-3	-4	-5	-6	-7	-8
I. Increasing racial equality........	38-1	-2	-3	-4	-5	-6	-7	-8
J. Greater equality for women........	39-1	-2	-3	-4	-5	-6	-7	-8
K. The separation of church and state...................	40-1	-2	-3	-4	-5	-6	-7	-8
L. Reducing United States dependence on other nations...................	41-1	-2	-3	-4	-5	-6	-7	-8

A & B 7. (HAND CARD B) Now I'd like to know how important you personally feel each of the following are. Again, on a scale of 1 to 7, where one is very important and seven is not very important. Let's start with A, where would it fall on the scale? (RECORD ONE ANSWER BELOW AND CONTINUE WITH LIST)

	1 Very Important	2	3	4	5	6	7 Not Very Important	Not Sure
A. Friendship................	42-1	-2	-3	-4	-5	-6	-7	-8
B. Money....................	43-1	-2	-3	-4	-5	-6	-7	-8
C. Patriotism..............	44-1	-2	-3	-4	-5	-6	-7	-8
D. Religion................	45-1	-2	-3	-4	-5	-6	-7	-8
E. Living a clean, moral life....	46-1	-2	-3	-4	-5	-6	-7	-8
F. Work....................	47-1	-2	-3	-4	-5	-6	-7	-8
G. Family..................	48-1	-2	-3	-4	-5	-6	-7	-8
H. Education...............	49-1	-2	-3	-4	-5	-6	-7	-8

DO NOT ASK RESPONDENTS ABOUT THEIR OWN ETHNIC GROUP IN Q.8a-12.
(SEE SCREENER)

Now I'd like to ask you a few questions about different groups in America like Black Americans, Italian Americans, Japanese Americans and so on.

A 8a. First of all, do you think of (READ FIRST GROUP ON LIST) as being more ambitious than other people, less ambitious or about the same? (RECORD ONE ANSWER BELOW AND CONTINUE WITH LIST)

	More Ambitious	Less Ambitious	About The Same	Don't Know
Blacks........................	50-1	-2	-3	-4
Italians......................	51-1	-2	-3	-4
Jews..........................	52-1	-2	-3	-4
Japanese......................	53-1	-2	-3	-4

A 8b. Do you think that on the average (READ FIRST GROUP ON LIST) have more money than most people, less money or about the same? (RECORD UNDER Q.8b AND CONTINUE WITH LIST)

8c. IF "MORE" MONEY IN Q.8b, ASK: Does it bother you at all that (name of group) have more money that most people (RECORD BELOW UNDER Q.8c AND CONTINUE WITH LIST)

	Q.8b				Q.8c		
	More	Less	Same	Not Sure	Yes	No	Not Sure
Blacks........................	54-1	-2	-3	-4	58-1	-2	-3
Italians......................	55-1	-2	-3	-4	59-1	-2	-3
Jews..........................	56-1	-2	-3	-4	60-1	-2	-3
Japanese......................	57-1	-2	-3	-4	61-1	-2	-3

A 9a. Do you think (READ FIRST GROUP ON LIST) are trying to push in where they are not wanted? (RECORD ONE ANSWER BELOW AND CONTINUE WITH LIST)

	Yes	No	Not Sure
Blacks........................	62-1	-2	-3
Italians......................	63-1	-2	-3
Jews..........................	64-1	-2	-3
Japanese......................	65-1	-2	-3

143

A   9b. Do you think (READ FIRST GROUP ON LIST) tend to be very family oriented or not that
        family oriented? (RECORD ONE ANSWER BELOW AND CONTINUE WITH LIST)

	Very Family Oriented	Not That Family Oriented	Not Sure
Blacks...........	66 -1	-2	-3
Italians.........	67 -1	-2	-3
Jews.............	68 -1	-2	-3
Japanese.........	69 -1	-2	-3

A   10a. Do you think that (READ FIRST GROUP ON LIST) have too much power in the United States?
        (RECORD ONE ANSWER BELOW AND CONTINUE WITH LIST)

	Yes	No	Not Sure
Blacks...........	70 -1	-2	-3
Italians.........	71 -1	-2	-3
Jews.............	72 -1	-2	-3
Japanese.........	73 -1	-2	-3

A   10b. How about in the business world, do you think (READ FIRST GROUP ON LIST) have too much
        power in the business world? (RECORD ONE ANSWER BELOW AND CONTINUE WITH LIST)

	Yes	No	Not Sure
Blacks...........	74 -1	-2	-3
Italians.........	75 -1	-2	-3
Jews.............	76 -1	-2	-3
Japanese.........	77 -1	-2	-3

80-1

144

A

10c. (HAND CARD C) Now I'd like you to look at this card and tell me in which of these areas, if any, (name of group) have too much influence? Just call off the letters. (GO THROUGH ENTIRE LIST FOR BLACKS, THEN CONTINUE WITH EACH GROUP) (MULTIPLE RECORD)

CARD 2

	Blacks	Italians	Jews	Japanese
A. Sports.....................	5 -1	21 -1	37-1	53 -1
B. Business...................	6 -1	22 -1	38-1	54 -1
C. Medicine...................	7 -1	23 -1	39-1	55 -1
D. Real estate................	8 -1	24 -1	40-1	56 -1
E. Politics...................	9 -1	25 -1	41-1	57 -1
F. Government in general......	10 -1	26 -1	42-1	58 -1
G. The movies.................	11 -1	27 -1	43-1	59 -1
H. Newspaper..................	12 -1	28 -1	44-1	60 -1
I. Banking....................	13 -1	29 -1	45-1	61 -1
J. Education..................	14 -1	30 -1	46-1	62 -1
K. Unions.....................	15 -1	31 -1	47-1	63 -1
L. The legal profession.......	16 -1	32 -1	48-1	64 -1
M. Other:	17 -1	33 -1	49-1	65 -1
None (VOLUNTEERED)(SPECIFY).....	18-1	34-1	50-1	66-1
	19-1	35-1	51-1	67-1

A

11a. Suppose you had a child who wanted to marry a (READ FIRST GROUP ON LIST) who had a good education and came from a good family. How would you feel about this -- would you object strongly, somewhat, a little, or not at all? (RECORD ONE ANSWER BELOW AND CONTINUE WITH LIST)

	Strongly	Somewhat	A Little	Not At All	Not Sure
Black......................	69-1	-2	-3	-4	-5
Italian....................	70-1	-2	-3	-4	-5
Jew........................	71-1	-2	-3	-4	-5
Japanese...................	72-1	-2	-3	-4	-5

145

A 1lb. How do you feel about having (READ FIRST GROUP ON LIST) in your neighborhood? Would you like to have some (name of group) neighbors, wouldn't it make any difference to you or would you prefer not to have any (name of group) neighbors? (RECORD ONE ANSWER BELOW AND CONTINUE WITH LIST)

	Like To Have Some	Wouldn't Make Any Difference	Prefer Not To Have Any	Not Sure
Blacks......	73-1	-2	-3	-4
Italians......	74-1	-2	-3	-4
Jews......	75-1	-2	-3	-4
Japanese......	76-1	-2	-3	-4

80-2

A 1lc. Suppose your political party wanted to nominate a (READ FIRST GROUP ON LIST) for President of the United States, would this disturb you very much, somewhat, very little, or not at all? (RECORD ONE ANSWER BELOW AND CONTINUE WITH LIST)

CARD 3

	Very Much	Some-what	Very Little	Not At All	Not Sure
Black......	5-1	-2	-3	-4	-5
Italian......	6-1	-2	-3	-4	-5
Jew......	7-1	-2	-3	-4	-5
Japanese......	8-1	-2	-3	-4	-5

A 12. At the present time, do you come into contact with (name of group) in any of the follo-wing ways. (READ ALL STATEMENTS FOR BLACKS, CIRCLE CODE IF "YES" AND THEN CONTINUE WITH EACH GROUP) (MULTIPLE RECORD)

	Black	Italian	Jew	Japanese
A. In your neighborhood?......	9-1	17-1	25-1	33-1
B. At work or in business?......	10-1	18-1	26-1	34-1
C. At stores you shop at?......	11-1	19-1	27-1	35-1
D. In clubs or organizations you belong to?...	12-1	20-1	28-1	36-1

146

E. Is your doctor or dentist (NAME OF GROUP)?   13 -1   21 -1   29 -1   37 -1

F. Have you ever had a close friend who was (NAME OF GROUP)?...............   14 -1   22 -1   30 -1   38 -1

G. Thinking of the eight or ten people you know best at the present time, are any of them (NAME OF GROUP)?...............   15 -1   23 -1   31 -1   39 -1

H. Is someone in your family married to a (NAME OF GROUP)...............   16 -1   24 -1   32 -1   40 -1

A   13a. (HAND CARD D) Now I'd like you to look at the list of statements about Jews. In each case please tell me whether you think the statement is probably true or probably false. Let's start with statement A, do you think it is probably true or probably false? (RECORD ONE ANSWER BELOW AND CONTINUE WITH LIST)

	Probably True	Probably False	Not Sure
Statement A.........	41 -1	-2	-3
Statement B.........	42 -1	-2	-3
Statement C.........	43 -1	-2	-3
Statement D.........	44 -1	-2	-3
Statement E.........	45 -1	-2	-3
Statement F.........	46 -1	-2	-3
Statement G.........	47 -1	-2	-3
Statement H.........	48 -1	-2	-3
Statement I.........	49 -1	-2	-3
Statement J.........	50 -1	-2	-3
Statement K.........	51 -1	-2	-3
Statement L.........	52 -1	-2	-3
Statement M.........	53 -1	-2	-3
Statement N.........	54 -1	-2	-3
Statement O.........	55 -1	-2	-3
Statement P.........	56 -1	-2	-3
Statement Q.........	57 -1	-2	-3
Statement R.........	58 -1	-2	-3
Statement S.........	59 -1	-2	-3

60-67=8

147

I'd like to ask you some questions about how you think the majority of non-Jews view Jews.

B   8a.   Do you think the majority of non-Jews think of Jews as being more ambitious than other people, less ambitious, or about the same?

More ambitious..........52-1
Less ambitious............. -2
About the same............. -3
Don't know................. -4

53-55 = g

B   8b.   Do you think that the majority of non-Jews think that on the average, Jews have more money than most people, less money or about the same?

More.....................56-1
Less....................... -2
Same....................... -3
Not sure................... -4

(SKIP TO Q.9)

57-59 = g

B   8c.   IF MORE IN Q.8b, ASK: Do you think the majority of non-Jews are bothered by their belief that Jews have more money than most people?

Yes.....................60-1
No......................... -2
Not sure................... -3

61-63 = g

B   9.   Do you think the majority of non-Jews think Jews are trying to push in where they are not wanted?

Yes.....................64-1
No......................... -2
Not sure................... -3

148

B 10a. Do you think the majority of non-Jews think that Jews have too much power in the United States?

65-71 = g

Yes.....................72-1
No......................-2
Not sure................-3

B 10b. Do you think the majority of non-Jews think that Jews have too much power in the business world?

73-75 = g

Yes.....................76-1
No......................-2
Not sure................-3

77 = g   80-1

B 10c. (HAND CARD C) Now I'd like you to look at this card and tell me which of these areas, if any, you think the majority of non-Jews think have too much influence? Just call off the letters.

CARD 2   5-36 = g

A. Sports....................37-1
B. Business..................38-2
C. Medicine..................39-3
D. Real estate...............40-4
E. Politics..................41-5
F. Government in general.....42-6
G. The movies................43-7
H. Newspapers................44-8
I. Banking...................45-9
J. Education.................46-0
K. Unions....................47-x
L. The legal profession......48-y
M. Other:....................49-1
         (SPECIFY)
    None......................50-2
                             51-1
                             52-1

B   11a.   How would the majority of non-Jews feel about having a child who wanted to
            marry a Jew who had a good education and came from a good family? Would they
            object strongly, somewhat, a little or not at all?

                                                                        53-70 = B

                                                   Strongly.. 71-1
                                                   Somewhat..   -2
                                                   A little..   -3
                                                   Not at all   -4
                                                   Don't know   -5

B   11b.   How would the majority of non-Jews feel about having Jews in their neighborhood?
            Do you think they would like to have some Jews, wouldn't it make any difference
            to them or would they prefer not to have any Jewish neighbors?
                                                                        72-74 = B

                                                   Like to have some........... 75-1
                                                   Wouldn't make any difference.. -2
                                                   Prefer not to have any.......   -3
                                                   Don't know...................   -4

                                                                        76 = B
                                                                             80-2

150

B

12. How do you think the majority of non-Jews would feel if their political party wanted to nominate a Jew for President of the United States -- do you think this would disturb them very much, somewhat, very little or not at all?

CARD 3   5 - 6 = B

Very much........ 7-1
Somewhat......... -2
Very little...... -3
Not at all....... -4
Don't know....... -5

8-59 = B

B

13. At the present time, do you come into contact with non-Jews in any of the following ways? (READ FIRST ITEM, RECORD ONE ANSWER, AND CONTINUE WITH LIST)

	Yes	No	Not Sure
A. In your neighborhood?......................................	60-1	-2	-3
B. At work or in business?...................................	61-1	-2	-3
C. At stores you shop at?....................................	62-1	-2	-3
D. In clubs or organizations you belong to?.................	63-1	-2	-3
E. Is your doctor or dentist not Jewish?....................	64-1	-2	-3
F. Have you ever had a close friend who was not Jewish?.....	65-1	-2	-3
G. Thinking of the 8 or 10 people you know best at the present time, are any of them not Jewish?.....................	66-1	-2	-3
H. Is someone in your family married to a non-Jew?.........	67-1	-2	-3

151

A & B   13b. Do you think Jews are losing their distinctive identity and becoming more like other
        Americans?

                                              Yes............ 68 -1
                                              No.............   -2
                                   (SKIP TO Q.14a) Not sure......   -3

A & B   13c. IF YES IN Q.13b, ASK: Do you think this is a good trend or not a good trend?

                                              Good trend........ 69 -1
                                              Not a good trend...   -2
                                              Not sure..........   -3

A & B   14a. (HAND CARD E) In the last year or two, have you seen any of the following kinds of
        incidents in your neighborhood or where you work? Just call off the numbers.

                                              1................ 70-1
                                              2................ 71-1
                                              3................ 72-1
                                              4................ 73-1
                                              5................ 74-1
                                              6................ 75-1

                                              7. Other: _____ 76-1
                                                           (SPECIFY)
                                   (SKIP TO Q.15a) -8. None............... 77-1
                                                                          78-1   80-

A & B   14b. Would you say that this sort of thing is happening less often than it did five or ten
        years ago, more often or about the same?

                                              CARD 4
                                              Less...... 5 -1
                                              More......   -2
                                              Same......   -3

152

A & B 15a. Do you see any possibility of an increase in this type of anti-semitism in this area? (RECORD BELOW UNDER Q.15a)

A & B 15b. How about elsewhere in the country, do you see the possibility of an increase in this type of anti-semitism elsewhere in the country? (RECORD BELOW UNDER Q.15b)

	15a	15b
Yes............	6 -1	7 -1
No.............	-2	-2
Not sure.......	-3	-3

A & B 16. IF YES IN Q.15a or b, ASK: Why do you say that -- what might cause an increase in anti-semitism?

```
8-
9-
10-
11-
12-
13-
14-
15-
16-
17-
18-
19-
```

A & B 17. Let me ask a few questions about Israel. First of all, do you think that it is very important that we continue to support Israel, somewhat important, or not important at all?

Very important............	20-1
Somewhat important........	-2
Not important at all......	-3
Not sure..................	-4

153

A & B 18. As you may know, the Israeli government has a treaty with Egypt, but has refused to negotiate with the Palestine Liberation Organization. Do you think that she is doing the right or wrong thing in refusing to negotiate with the Palestinian Liberation Organization?

Right thing...... 21-1
Wrong thing...... -2
Not sure......... -3

A & B 19. Do you feel that the continuation of Israel as a Jewish state is important or not important to our country and people like yourself?

Important........ 22-1
Not important.... -2
Not sure......... -3

A & B 20a. Many Israelis are fearful about a plan to set up a Palestinian State on their West Bank, even if the United States guarantees Israel's security. Do you think the Israelis are being reasonable or unreasonable in taking this attitude?

Reasonable....... 23-1
Unreasonable..... -2
Not sure......... -3

A & B 20b. Do you think Israel has the right to make Jerusalem the capital of Israel?

Yes............. 24-1
No.............. -2
Not sure....... -3
                25=B

A & B 21a. In view of the situation in the Middle East, do you feel that the U.S. should increase its present military aid to Israel, continue it at the same level as now, or cut it back?

Increase......... 26-1
Same............. -2
Cut it back...... -3
Not sure......... -4

154

B   21b.   Many Israelis are fearful about giving back to the Arabs some of the territory they won in previous wars, such as the Golan Heights. They say that without the Golan Heights they will not be able to protect their borders against an attack by Syria. Do you think that the Israelis are being reasonable or unreasonable in taking this attitude?

Reasonable......... 25-1
Unreasonable....... -2
Not sure........... -3

A & B   22a.   Have you heard or read about the relations between the Jews in Israel and the Arab refugees there?

Yes...... 27-1
No....... -2
(SKIP TO Q.23)

A & B   22b.   IF YES IN Q.22a, ASK: As far as you know, have Arabs in Israel been treated very well, pretty well, pretty badly, or very badly?

Very well.......... 28-1
Pretty well........ -2
Pretty badly....... -3
Very badly......... -4
Not sure........... -5

A & B   23.   Suppose there were a war between the Arab nation and Israel. Which side do you think you would probably sympathize with?

Arab nations...... 29-1
Israel............. -2
Neither........... -3
Not sure.......... -4

A & B   24a.   Do you think that most Jewish people in this country feel closer to the United States or to Israel?

United States...... 30-1
Israel............. -2
Both (VOLUNTEERED).. -3
Not sure........... -4

155

A & B   24b.   If the U.S. and Israel ever broke off relations, with whom do you think most American Jews would side in the dispute?

United States......... 31 -1
Israel................ -2
Both (VOLUNTEERED).... -3
Not sure.............. -4
32=B

A   24c.   Has the existence of the State of Israel made you think more highly of American Jews, less highly or hasn't it affected your opinion one way or the other?

More highly..........33 -1
Less highly.......... -2
Hasn't affected opinion...... -3
Not sure............. -4

B   24d.   **Has the existence of the State of Israel made you more proud of being Jewish, less proud, or hasn't it affected your feelings one way or another?**

More proud...........32-1
Less proud........... -2
Hasn't affected opinion.... -3
Not sure............ -4
33 = B

Now I'd like to ask you a few questions about your own religious beliefs.

A & B   25.   (HAND RESPONDENT CARD F)   Please look at this card and tell me which statement comes closest to expressing what you believe about God.   Just call off the number.   (RECORD ONE ANSWER)

1.   I don't believe in God..................................... 34 -1
2.   I don't know whether there is a God and I don't believe there is any way to find out...... -2
3.   I don't believe in a personal God, but I do believe in a higher power of some kind...... -3
4.   I find myself believing in God some of the time, but not at other times..... -4
5.   While I have doubts, I feel that I do believe in God..... -5
6.   I know God really exists and I have no doubts about it..... -6
     Not sure..... -7

156

A   26. We've heard a lot in the last few years about individuals who have been "born again" -- have you personally had such an experience?

```
                                              Yes............ 35 -1
                                              No.................  -2
                                              Not sure......  -3
                                              No answer......  -4
```

A   27a. Do you think that a person who doesn't accept Jesus can be saved?

```
                                              Yes............ 36 -1
                                              No.................  -2

                                              Other: _____  -3
                                                   (SPECIFY)
                                              Not sure...........  -4
```

A   27b. Some people believe that the reason Jews have so much trouble is because God is punishing them for rejecting Jesus. Do you agree with this?

```
                                              Yes............ 37 -1
                                              No.................  -2
                                              Not sure......  -3
```

A   28. What about the belief that the Devil actually exists? Are you absolutely sure or are you pretty sure that the Devil exists or are you absolutely sure or pretty sure that the Devil does not exist?

```
                            Absolutely sure there is a devil.... 38 -1
                            Pretty sure there is a devil........  -2
                            Absolutely sure there is no devil..  -3
                            Pretty sure there is no devil......  -4
                            Not sure.............................  -5
```

A   29. How sure are you that there is a life beyond death? Are you absolutely sure or pretty
          sure that there is a life beyond death or are you absolutely or pretty sure that there
          is no life beyond death?

                    Absolutely sure there is a life beyond
                       death.......................... 39 -1
                    Pretty sure there is a life beyond death.. -2
                    Absolutely sure there is no life beyond
                       death.............................. -3
                    Pretty sure there is no life beyond death. -4
                    Not sure........................... -5

A & B 30. All in all, how important would you say religion is to you—extremely important,
            quite important, fairly important, not too important, or not important at all?

                    Extremely important........ 40 -1
                    Quite important............ -2
                    Fairly important........... -3
                    Not too important.......... -4
                    Not important at all....... -5
                    Not sure................... -6

A & B 31a. Suppose someone admitted in public that he didn't believe in God. Do you think he or
            she should be allowed to teach in a public high school?

                    Yes........... 41 -1
                    No............ -2
                    Not sure...... -3

A & B 31b. Should he or she be allowed to hold public office?

                    Yes........... 42 -1
                    No............ -2
                    Not sure...... -3

A & B 31c. Do you think that a book he or she wrote should be removed from a public library?

Yes..........43 -1
No............. -2
Not sure....... -3

A & B 32. How do you feel about prayers being said in the public schools -- are you strongly in favor, somewhat in favor, somewhat opposed, or strongly opposed?

Strongly in favor....... 44-1
Somewhat in favor....... -2
Somewhat opposed........ -3
Strongly opposed........ -4
Don't know.............. -5

CLASSIFICATION DATA

A. What was your age on your last birthday?

      18-24........................ 45 -1
      25-29........................   -2
      30-34........................   -3
      35-39........................   -4
      40-54........................   -5
      55-64........................   -6
      65 and over..................   -7

B. Are you single, married, divorced, sepa-
   rated, or widowed?

      Single....................... 46 -1
      Presently married............   -2
      Separated....................   -3
      Divorced.....................   -4
      Widowed......................   -5

C. For the most part, were you raised on a
   farm, in a small town, in a medium-sized
   city, a big city, or a suburb of a big
   city?

      Farm......................... 47 -1
      Small town...................   -2
      Small city...................   -3
      Medium-sized city............   -4
      Big city.....................   -5
      Suburb to a big city.........   -6
      Don't know...................   -7

E4. What is your position in your household?

      Male head.................... 52 -1
      Wife.........................   -2
      Female head (no male)........   -3
      Son..........................   -4
      Daughter.....................   -5
      Other........................   -6

F1. What is your occupation? (WRITE IN
    UNDER F1 AND RECORD BELOW)

F2. IF NOT HEAD OF HOUSEHOLD: What is the
    occupation of the head of household?
    (WRITE IN UNDER F2 AND RECORD BELOW)

F1 _____

F2 _____

	F1 Respon-dent	F2 Household Head
Professional/exec-utive/owner.....	53-1	54-1
White collar......	-2	-2
Blue collar.......	-3	-3
Retired...........	-4	-4
Unemployed........	-5	-5
Student...........	-6	-6
Housewife.........	-7	-7

D. About how many years have you lived in (name of city or town currently reside in)?

```
Less than 1 year................  48-1
1 up to less than 2 years.......    -2
2 up to less than 3 years.......    -3
3 up to less than 6 years.......    -4
6 up to less than 10 years......    -5
10 up to less than 20 years.....    -6
20 up to less than 30 years.....    -7
30 years or more................    -8
Don't know......................    -9
```

E1. What is the last grade of school you completed? (RECORD BELOW UNDER Q.E1)

E2. What was the last grade of school your father completed? (RECORD BELOW UNDER Q.E2)

E3. What was the last grade of school your mother completed? (RECORD BELOW UNDER Q.E3)

	E1	E2	E3
Less than high school graduate.......... 49-1	50-1	51-1
High school graduate.....	-2	-2	-2
Some college...........	-3	-3	-3
College graduate/post graduate.........	-4	-4	-4
Not sure/No answer (VOLUNTEERED)...........	-5	-5	-5

G1. What is your religion? (READ LIST)

```
(ASK GA)  - Protestant..........55 -1
(ASK GB1) - Catholic.............    -2
(ASK GC1) - Jewish...............    -3

(SKIP TO
 Q.H)     - Other:_____    -4

(SKIP TO
 Q.I)     - None................    -5
```

GA. (IF PROTESTANT) What denomination is that?

```
Adventist......................56 -1
Baptist........................    -2
Congregationalist..............    -3
Episcopalian...................    -4
Lutheran.......................    -5
Methodist......................    -6
Morman.........................    -7
Pentecostal....................    -8
Presbyterian...................    -9
Unitarian......................    -0
United Church of Christ........    -x

Other:_____      -y
                           57-
```

GB1. (IF CATHOLIC) Have you ever attended a parochial school.
       Yes..... 58-1
       No......   -2
       (SKIP TO Q.H)

GB2. IF YES IN GB1, ASK: How many years did you attend?
      59-
      60-_____ years

GC1 (IF JEWISH) Do you think of yourself as being Orthodox, Conservative, Reformed, or just Jewish?

Orthodox..................... 61 -1
Conservative................. -2
Reformed..................... -3
Just Jewish.................. -4

GC2 Are you affiliated with a synagogue?

Yes.......................... 62 -1
No........................... -2

H. About how often do you attend worship services? (CIRCLE CODE FOR CATEGORY THAT COMES CLOSEST)

Several times a week......... 63 -1
Every week................... -2
Nearly every week............ -3
2-3 times a month............ -4
About once a month........... -5
Several times a year......... -6
About once or twice a year... -7
Less than once a year........ -8
Never........................ -9
Not sure..................... -0

I. Are you a (READ LIST)?

Democrat..................... 64 -1
Republican................... -2
Independent.................. -3
Other........................ -4
Not registered............... -5

K. (HAND CARD G) Which of these magazines do you read regularly or subscribe to? Just call off the numbers.
CARD 5

1........	5 -1		14.......	18 -1
2........	6 -1		15.......	19 -1
3........	7 -1		16.......	20 -1
4........	8 -1		17.......	21 -1
5........	9 -1		18.......	22 -1
6........	10 -1		19.......	23 -1
7........	11 -1		20.......	24 -1
8........	12 -1		21.......	25 -1
9........	13 -1		22.......	26 -1
10.......	14 -1		23.......	27 -1
11.......	15 -1		24.......	28 -1
12.......	16 -1		25.......	29 -1
13.......	17 -1		26.......	30 -1
			27.......	31 -1

28 Other:

_____ 32-1
(SPECIFY)
None......... 33-1
             34-1
             35-1

L. (HAND CARD H) In what category on this card does your total family income fall? Just read me the letter beside the amount.

A........... 36 -1   E............. -5
B........... -2   F............. -6
C........... -3   G............. -7
D........... -4   H............. -8
                     Refused....... -9

J1. Regardless of your political affiliation
-- do you think of yourself as being
conservative, moderate, liberal or
radical?

Conservative............ 65 -1
Moderate................   -2
Liberal.................   -3
Radical.................   -4

J2. In the last few years would you say you
have become more conservative, more liberal, more radical or haven't you
changed much either way?

More conservative....... 66 -1
More liberal............   -2
More radical............   -3
Haven't changed.........   -4
Not sure (VOLUNTEERED)..   -5

J3. In the recent presidential election, did
you vote for Carter the Democrat, Reagan
the Republican, Anderson the Independent
or someone else?

Carter.................. 67 -1
Reagan..................   -2
Anderson................   -3
Other...................   -4
Didn't vote/not registered.......   -5

80-4

M. (HAND CARD I) Which of these types of
groups, if any, are you personally
active in? (JUST READ THE NUMBER ON
THE CARD)

1............... 37 -1   8......... 44 -1
2............... 38 -1   9......... 45 -1
3............... 39 -1   10......... 46 -1
4............... 40 -1   11......... 47 -1
5............... 41 -1   12......... 48 -1
6............... 42 -1   13......... 49 -1
7............... 43 -1   14......... 50 -1
                           15......... 51 -1
                         None......... 52 -1

N1. By and large, do you think of yourself
as being of the upper class, upper middle class; middle class, or lower class?
(RECORD BELOW UNDER Q.N1)

N2. Thinking back to the time you were growing up, would you say that your family
was of the upper class, upper middle
class, middle class, or lower class?
(RECORD BELOW UNDER Q.N2)

	N1	N2
Upper...............	53 -1	54 -1
Upper middle........	-2	-2
Middle..............	-3	-3
Lower...............	-4	-4
Don't know..........	-5	-5

O. (HAND CARD J) Finally, I'd like you to read the statements on this card and for each one tell me if you agree or disagree.

	Agree	Disagree	Not Sure
Statement A......	55-1	-2	-3
B......	56-1	-2	-3
C......	57-1	-2	-3
D......	58-1	-2	-3
E......	59-1	-2	-3
F......	60-1	-2	-3
G......	61-1	-2	-3

RECORD -- DO NOT ASK

Sex:

Male............................ 62-1
Female.......................... -2

White........................... 63-1
Black........................... -2
Oriental........................ -3
Hispanic........................ -4
Other _____ -5
      (SPECIFY)

Interviewer Data: To be filled out by and about interviewer.

Your age:
18-24........................... 64-1
25-29........................... -2
30-34........................... -3
35-39........................... -4
40-54........................... -5
55-64........................... -6
65 and over..................... -7

Your sex:

Male............................ 65-1
Female.......................... -2

Your religion:

Catholic........................ 66-1
Protestant...................... -2
Jewish.......................... -3
Other _____
      (SPECIFY)
None............................ -5

BIBLIOGRAPHY

BOOKS AND MONOGRAPHS

Adorno, T. W., et al. *The Authoritarian Personality* (New York: W. W. Norton, 1950).

Baldwin, James. "Negroes Are Anti-Semitic because They're Anti-White." In *Anti-Semitism in The United States*, L. Dinnerstein, ed. (New York: Holt, Rinehart & Winston, 1971), pp. 125–131.

Bettelheim, Bruno, and Janowitz, Morris. *Dynamics of Prejudice: A Psychological and Sociological Study of Veterans* (New York: Harper & Row, 1950).

Bogardus, E. S. *Immigration and Race Attitudes* (Boston: D. C. Heath, 1928).

Brown, Roger. *Social Psychology* (New York: Free Press, 1965).

Caplovitz, David, and Rogers, Candace. *Swastika 1960: The Epidemic of Anti-Semitic Vandalism in America* (New York: Anti-Defamation League of B'nai B'rith, 1960).

Fishbein, M. "The Relationship between Attitudes and Behavior." In *Cognitive Consistency*, S. Feldman, ed. (New York: Academic Press, 1966).

Forster, Arnold, and Epstein, Benjamin. *The New Anti-Semitism*. New York: McGraw Hill, 1974.

Gallup Organization. *Religion in America*, 1981.

Glazer, Nathan and Moynihan, Daniel Patrick. *Beyond the Melting Pot* (Cambridge: MIT Press, 1964).

Glock, Charles, Selznick, Gertrude, and Spaeth, Joseph. *The Apathetic Majority: A Study Based on Public Response to the Eichmann Trial* (New York: Harper & Row, 1966).

——, and Stark, Rodney. *Christian Beliefs and Anti-Semitism* (New York: Harper and Row, 1966).

——. et al. *Adolescent Prejudice* (New York: Harper & Row, 1975).

Harris, Louis, and Associates. *A Study of Attitudes toward Racial and Religious Minorities and toward Women.* Conducted for the National Conference of Christians and Jews, New York, 1978.

———. *A Survey of the Attitudes of Americans toward the Arab-Israeli Conflict and toward American Jews*, New York, 1975.

Jones, E. E. et al. *Attribution: Perceiving the Causes of Behavior* (Morristown, N.J.: General Learning Press, 1972).

Lipset, Seymour Martin, and Raab, Earl. *The Politics of Unreason: Right Wing Extremism in America 1880-1970* (New York: Harper & Row, 1970).

Magnusson, David. *Test Theory* (Reading, Mass.: Addison-Wesley, 1966).

Marx, Gary. *Protest and Prejudice: A Study of Belief in the Black Community* (New York: Harper & Row, 1967).

Novak, Michael. *The Rise of the Unmeltable Ethnics* (New York: MacMillan, 1971).

Park, Robert. *Race and Culture* (Glencoe, Ill.: Free Press, 1955).

Quinley, Harold, and Glock, Charles. *Anti-Semitism in America* (New York: Harper & Row, 1979).

Radzinowicz, Leon, and Wolfgang, Marvin. *Crime and Justice* (New York: Basic Books, 1971).

Selznick, Gertrude, and Steinberg, Stephen. *The Tenacity of Prejudice* (New York: Harper & Row, 1969).

Stark, R. et al. *Wayward Sheperds: Prejudice and the Protestant Clergy* (New York: Harper & Row, 1971).

Stember, Charles Herbert, et al. *Jews in the Mind of America* (New York: Basic Books, 1966).

"Uniform Crime Reports—1968/U.S. Department of Justice." In *Crime and Justice*, vol. 1, Leon Radzinowicz and Marvin E. Wolfgang, eds. (New York: Basic Books, 1971, pp. 131-166).

U.S. Chamber of Commerce. *Statistical Abstract of the United States: 1980.* (Washington, D.C.: Government Printing Office, 1980).

Yankelovich, Daniel. *New Rules* (New York: Simon & Schuster, 1981).

JOURNALS AND PERIODICALS

Auden, W. H. "America is Not a Melting Pot." New York *Times Magazine*, April 16, 1972, p. 14.

Friedman, David. "The Disease Is Still Malignant." Brookline, Mass., *Jewish Times*, August 27, 1981.

Glock, Charles, and Stark, Rodney. "Do Christian Beliefs Cause Anti-Semitism: A Comment." *American Sociological Review* 38 (1973): 59-61.

Himmelfarb, Milton. "Are Jews Becoming More Republican?" *Commentary* 72 (August 1981): 27-31.

Kahle, Lynn, Klingel, David, and Kulka, Richard. "A Longitudinal Study of Adolescents' Attitude—Behavior Consistency." *Public Opinion Quarterly*, Fall 1981, pp. 402-414.

La Pierre, R. T. "Attitudes Versus Actions." *Social Forces* 13 (1934): 230-37.

Middleton, Russell. "Do Christian Beliefs Cause Anti-Semitism?" *American Sociological Review* 38 (1973): 33-52.

New York *Times*. "In a Troubled Poland, Jews Again seem to be Made Scapegoats," January 9, 1981, p. 6.

New York *Times*. "Feelings Toward Jews Found More Favorable In A Survey By Gallup," April 7, 1981.

"1981 Audit of Anti-Semitic Incidents." (New York: Anti-Defamation League of B'nai B'rith) mimeographed, p. 4.

"The Polls: Abortion." *Public Opinion Quarterly*, Winter 1977-78, pp. 553-564.

"The Polls: Changing Attitudes Toward Euthanasia." *Public Opinion Quarterly*, Spring 1980, pp. 123-128.

"The Polls: Homosexuality." *Public Opinion Quarterly*, Summer 1977, pp. 265-276.

"The Polls: Women At Work." *Public Opinion Quarterly*, Summer 1977, pp. 268–277.

"Racial Attitudes: Tensions Relax," *Public Opinion*, October/November 1980, pp. 28–29.

Roof, Wade Clark. "Religious Orthodoxy and Minority Prejudice: Causal Relationship or Reflection of Localistic World View?" *American Journal of Sociology* 80 (1974): 643–664.

Schneider, William. "Anti-Semitism and Israel: A Report on American Public Opinion." Mimeographed, December 1978.

Wicker, Allan. "Attitudes Versus Action: The Relationship of Verbal and Overt Behavioral Responses to Attitudes Objects." *Journal of Social Issues* 25 (1969): 25.

Yankelovich, Daniel. "Stepchildren of the Moral Majority." *Psychology Today*, November 1981, pp. 5–10.

INDEX

ABOUT THE AUTHORS

RUTH CLARK is a senior vice president with Yankelovich, Skelly and White, Inc. and Director of its Public Opinion Division. Prior to joining Yankelovich, Skelly and White, Inc., Mrs. Clark was a senior vice president with Louis Harris and Associates.

GREGORY MARTIRE is a vice president in the Public Opinion Division of Yankelovich, Skelly and White, Inc. Dr. Martire has written on a variety of subjects; his articles have appeared in *Psychiatric Opinion, Public Opinion,* and *Family Planning Perspectives.* Dr. Martire holds a Ph.D. from the University of Pennsylvania.